Zu Zweit

PAIR-WORK EXERCISES IN GERMAN

STUDENT'S BOOK 2

David Phillips

HODDER AND STOUGHTON
LONDON SYDNEY AUCKLAND TORONTO

Acknowledgments

I am grateful to Michèle Stubbs, Kate Morrall, and Louise McClelland for several ideas for pair work activities which have been incorporated in *Zu Zweit* and to Becky and Janet Phillips for similar help. I am indebted to Elisabeth Bolshaw of Hodder & Stoughton for her efficient help and encouragement throughout the period during which the books were written and to Margit Becher for checking the typescript.

The author and publishers would also like to thank the Werbe- und Verkehrsamt der Bundeshauptstadt Bonn for the map used in A1 and B1; the BVG for the plan of the Berlin underground used in A7; the Kölner Stadt-Anzeiger for the TV programmes (15.4.84) used in A11 and B11; the Hotel Kempinski for the hotel document used in A22 and B22; Berolina Stadtrundfahrten for the tour routes used in A24 and B24; and the *Sunday Times* for the map of Munich from *Nairn's Guide to Munich and Southern Bavaria*, used in A29 and B29.

British Library Cataloguing in Publication Data
Phillips, David, *1944 Dec. 15–*
  Zu Zweit.
  Pupils bk. 2
  1. German language—Composition and
  exercises
  I. Title
  438.3'421   PF3420

  ISBN 0-340-39150-2

First published 1986
Second impression 1989

Copyright © 1986 David Phillips

All rights reserved. No part of this publication may be reproduced or transmitted in any form or by any means, electronic or mechanical, including photocopy, recording, or any information storage and retrieval system, without permission in writing from the publisher or under licence from the Copyright Licensing Agency Limited. Further details of such licences (for reprographic reproduction) may be obtained from the Copyright Licensing Agency Limited, of 19 Bedford Square, London WC1.

Printed in Great Britain
for Hodder and Stoughton Educational
a division of Hodder and Stoughton Ltd, Mill Road
Dunton Green, Sevenoaks, Kent by
St Edmundsbury Press Ltd, Bury St Edmunds

Introduction

Zu Zweit is designed to provide oral practice in German for students working together in pairs. Student's Book 1 contains easier straightforward exercises suitable for beginners and some help with vocabulary, grammar and syntax; Student's Book 2 provides practice at a more advanced level. There is an accompanying Teacher's Book which contains copiable versions of documents from both books on which pupils can write (forms to complete, timetables to fill in, checklists, etc.), as well as suggestions on how the material might be used in the classroom.

Each exercise is designed in such a way as to provide all the necessary information for students to be able to complete the tasks set (in Book 1 this includes linguistic information), though some preliminary work will be necessary in a lot of cases.

It is hoped that *Zu Zweit* will encourage a communicative approach to the teaching of German that will result in greater confidence and fluency among both beginners and more advanced learners.

David Phillips
Oxford

STUDENT A   STUDENT A   STUDENT A   STUDENT A   STUDENT A

Looking for a hotel

A1

You have just arrived at the main station in Bonn and need to find a hotel room with shower for two nights. Ring the Information Office and ask about the availability of rooms. You will be told which hotels still have vacancies. Ask how to get to each of them and mark them on your map.

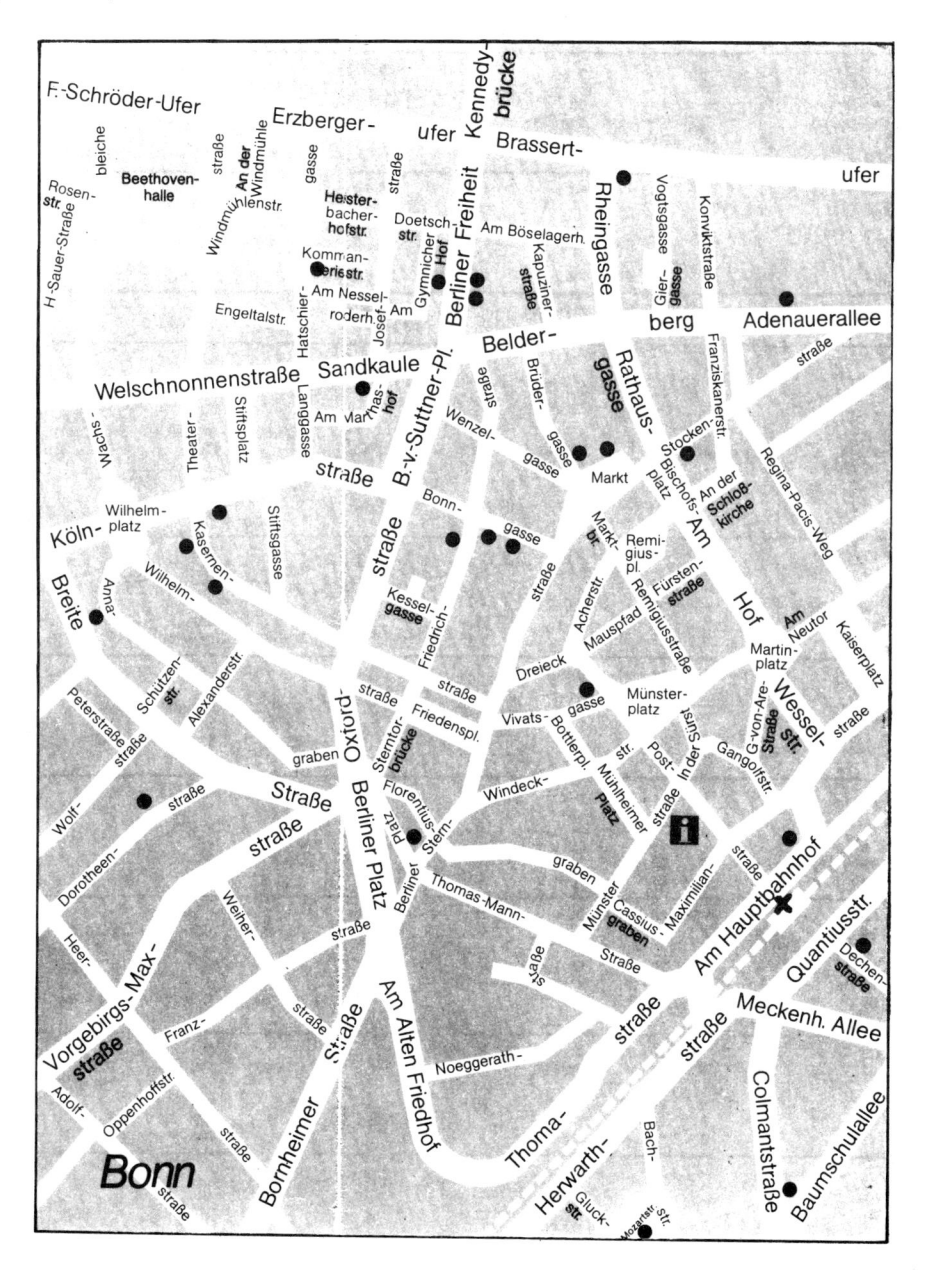

STUDENT A   STUDENT A   STUDENT A   STUDENT A   STUDENT A

A2 A robbery witnessed

You have just been a witness to a robbery at a jeweller's shop in Frankfurt. As you were walking past you saw a man run to his car clutching a bag full of silver and drive off in the direction of the airport. You now describe the scene to the police.

STUDENT A   STUDENT A   STUDENT A   STUDENT A   STUDENT A

Hunt-the-thimble

A3

Below is a sketch of a sitting room. Play a version of 'Hunt-the-thimble' with your partner. You decide where to hide a small object in the room and your partner has to guess where and what it is. You begin, then take it in turns.

STUDENT A   STUDENT A   STUDENT A   STUDENT A   STUDENT A

A4 A guessing game

Choose one of the people pictured below. Your partner will ask you questions to enable him/her to guess which face you have chosen.

When your partner has identified the correct face it is his/her turn to choose somebody and your turn to guess which face has been chosen.

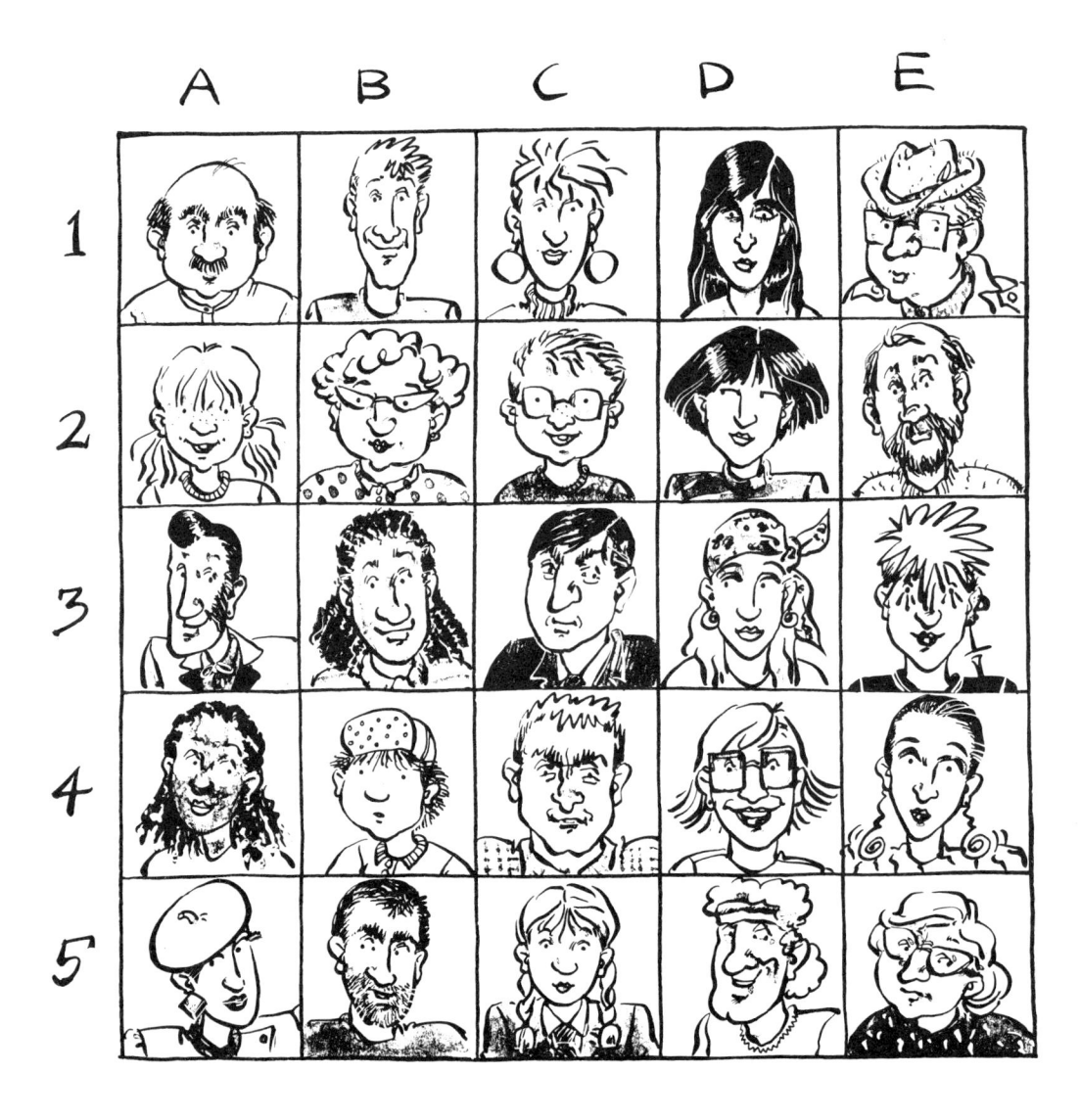

A spoilt menu

A5

STUDENT A   STUDENT A   STUDENT A   STUDENT A   STUDENT A

You and your friend are in a restaurant in Düsseldorf. You decide to choose something from the chef's special menu, but unfortunately previous diners have spilt coffee over your copy, obscuring some of the details. Ask your friend to supply the missing information. Your friend has similar problems. You begin.

ZUM GOLDENEN OCHSEN

Unser Küchenchef empfiehlt:

200	Putenbruststeak "Indische Art" mit geb. Früchten, Butterreis und grünem Salat	
201	Hamburger Krustentiersuppe mit Sahnehaube	DM 6,25

VORSPEISEN

202	Matjesröllchen "Lord - Nelson" auf Apfelring, gefüllt mit Sahnemeerrettich und Preiselbeeren, dazu Vollkornbrot und Butter	
203	Tatar vom Silberlachs mit Kräutermeerrettich,	DM 15,25
204	Toast "Wellington" kleines Rinderfilet mit Roquefortbirne überbacken	DM 18,00

HAUPTGERICHTE

205	Rinderleber "Berliner Art" mit Röstzwiebeln, Apfelringen, dazu Kartoffelmus und gemischter Salat	DM 17,75
206	"Ossobuco" Kalbsbeinscheiben mit Tomaten geschmort auf Spaghetti, dazu grüner Salat	DM 20,25
207	Schweinefilet "Kaukasische Art" mit Letcho-Gemüse und Pommes frites	DM 23,50
208	Kalbsnierenscheiben in Dijonersenfcreme auf Blattspinat und Sahnekartoffeln	DM
209	Rumpsteak "Westmoreland" mit Essiggemüse und Röstkartoffeln	DM 24,50
210	Aal grün in Dillrahmsauce mit Butterkartoffeln und Gurkensalat	DM 22,75
211	Ochsenlendenstück in Schneckensauce mit Zucchinischeiben und Schneekartoffeln	DM 28,75

DES

212	Grand Marnier und Vanilleeis	DM 8,75

In obigen Preisen sind Bedienung und gesetzl. MwSt. enthalten.

STUDENT A   STUDENT A   STUDENT A   STUDENT A   STUDENT A

A6 The ideal timetable

You are a reporter with a local radio station working on a programme on pupils' attitudes to school. You decide to ask one of your interviewees what his/her ideal school timetable would look like. Ask him/her to fill in a blank timetable, deciding on times of lessons, length of break, times at which school would begin and end each day, and what subjects would be studied. When your interviewee has completed the timetable ask for full details and enter them on your copy of the blank timetable.

STUNDENPLAN Klasse_____ Sommer/Winter-Halbjahr 19____

ZEIT	MONTAG	DIENSTAG	MITTWOCH	DONNERSTAG	FREITAG	SONNABEND

Your interviewee will now turn the tables on you and ask you to design *your* ideal school timetable. Fill in the blank timetable below and answer questions that will enable the interviewee to reconstruct it.

STUNDENPLAN Klasse_____ Sommer/Winter-Halbjahr 19____

ZEIT	MONTAG	DIENSTAG	MITTWOCH	DONNERSTAG	FREITAG	SONNABEND

STUDENT A   STUDENT A   STUDENT A   STUDENT A   STUDENT A

The Berlin Underground

A7

You work at an information desk in the Berlin Underground. A passenger will ask you to explain how he/she can travel between various stations in the network. Using the plan below, explain at which stations he/she must change in each case. The passenger will make a note of the details and will check them back with you.

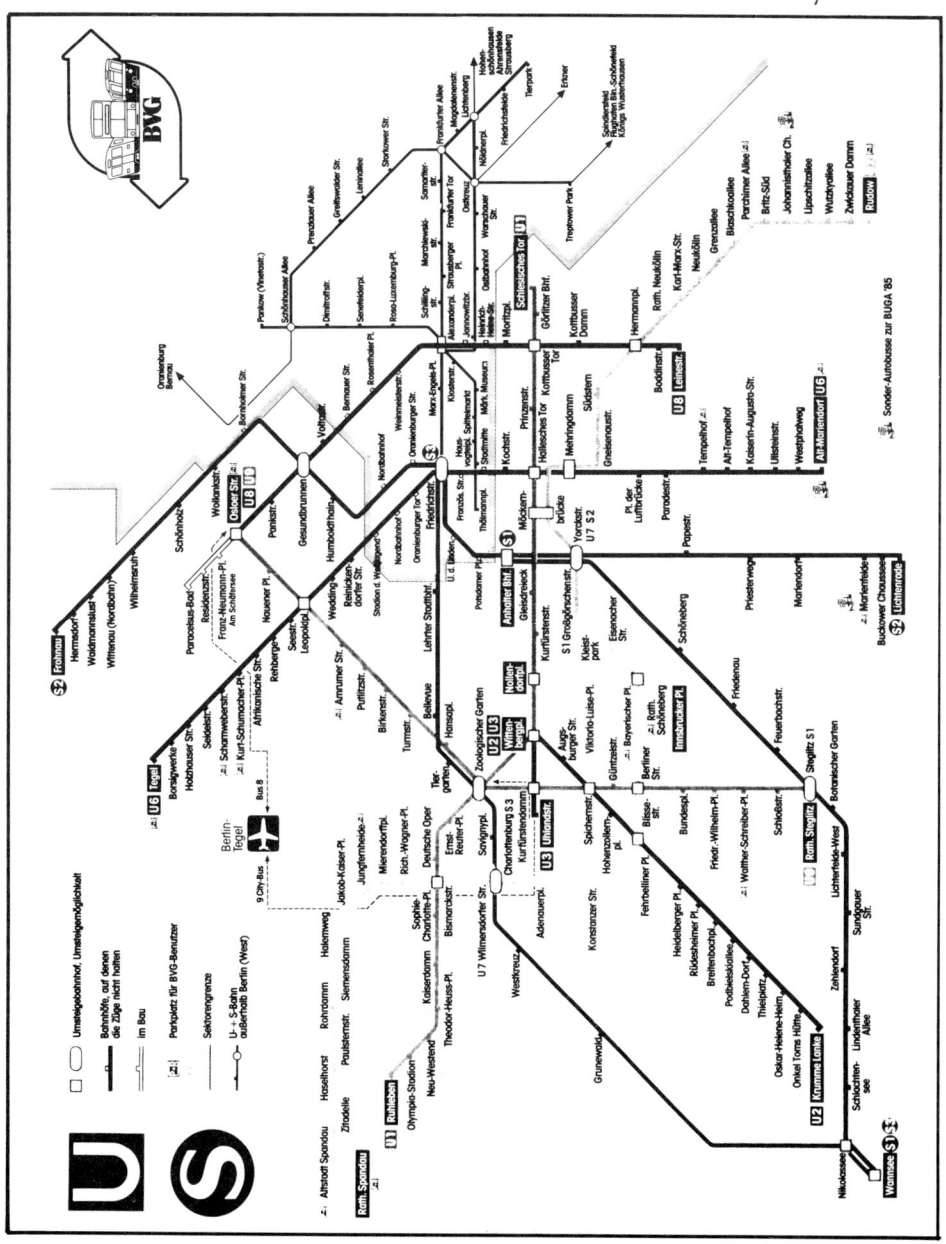

STUDENT A   STUDENT A   STUDENT A   STUDENT A   STUDENT A

A8 A burgled flat

While your neighbours, the Kellermann family, are away on holiday you have agreed to keep an eye on their flat. When you open the door to see if everything is all right you are horrified to discover that there has been a burglary and that lots of items are missing. You ring the Kellermann's at their holiday address and ask them to describe what was in the sitting room of the flat. Tell them which items are still there and which are now missing.

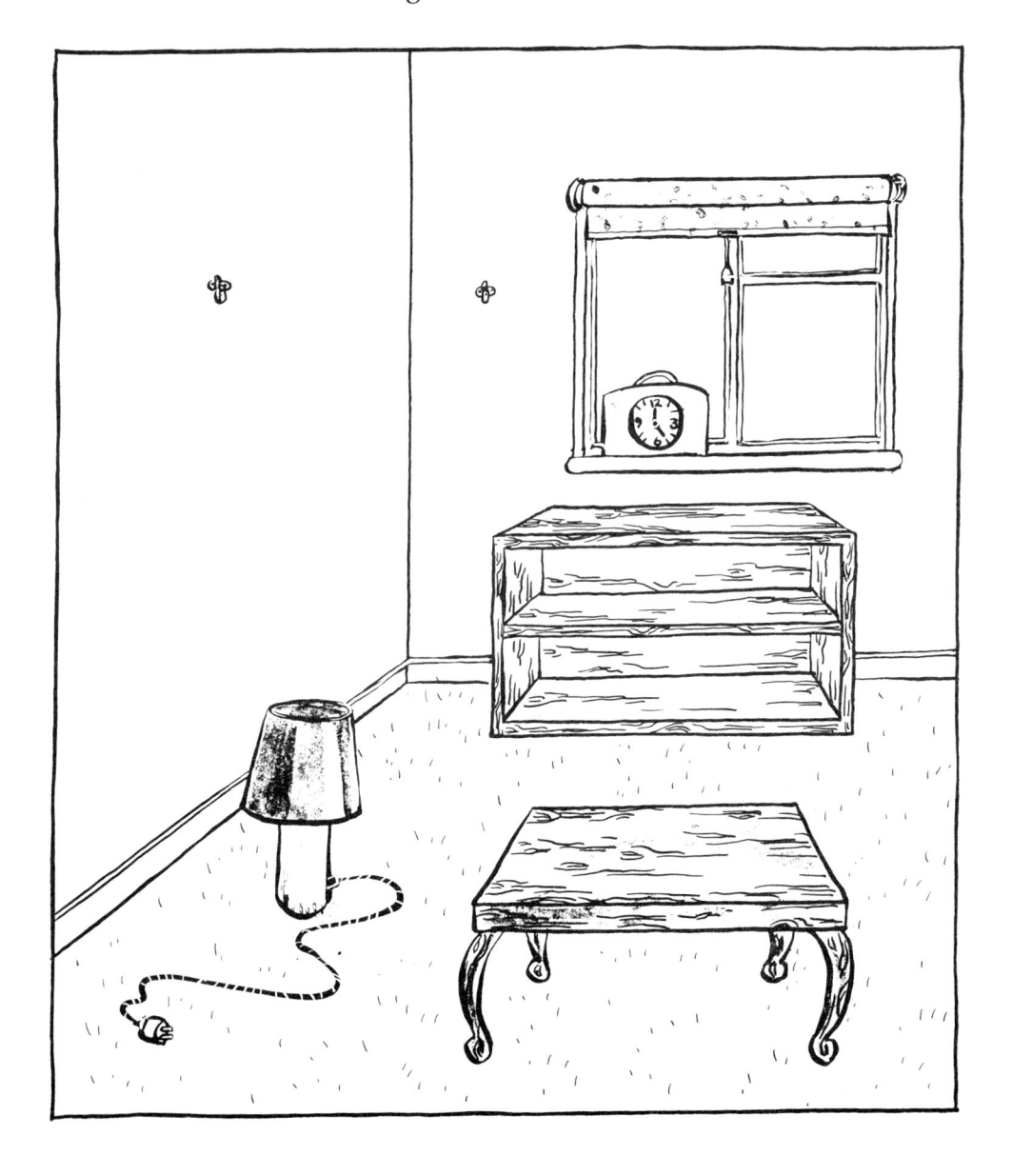

STUDENT A   STUDENT A   STUDENT A   STUDENT A   STUDENT A

Choosing a holiday

A9

You have a week's holiday due to you and can manage to get away some time in August. You decide that you want to visit an interesting foreign city. Discuss with your travel agent what holidays are available at a price you can afford (roughly DM 500). Make a note of the details and then decide which holiday to take.

A10 Ordering drinks

You are entertaining a group of 12 visitors and take them to a local bar-restaurant for drinks. Call the waiter/waitress over and order 13 drinks in all from the *Getränkekarte*. The waiter/waitress will write down your order and tell you the amount due. Check the sum with him/her by going through the drinks ordered and comparing the prices on his/her list.

Biere vom Faß
Schultheiß Pilsener	0,2 l	2,10
Schultheiß Pilsener	0,4 l	4,20
König Pilsener	0,2 l	2,50
König Pilsener	0,4 l	5,00

Flaschenbiere
Schultheiß Pilsener	0,33 l	4,10
Schultheiß Malz	0,33 l	3,50
Weizenbier	0,50 l	5,50
Diät Pils	0,33 l	4,50

Erfrischungen
Tonic-Water Schweppes	Fl. 0,2 l	3,75
Bitter-Lemon	Fl. 0,2 l	3,75
Coca-Cola	Fl. 0,2 l	3,25
Fanta Orange	Fl. 0,2 l	3,25
Apfelsaft	Fl. 0,2 l	3,75
Orangensaft	Fl. 0,2 l	4,00
Tomatensaft	Fl. 0,2 l	4,00

Warme Getränke
Tasse Kaffee	2,25
Kännchen Kaffee	4,50
Glas Tee	2,25
Kännchen Tee	4,50
Tasse Schokolade	2,50
Glas Glühwein	5,50
Glas Grog von 4 cl Rum	7,00

Schoppenweine (0,2 l)
Mosel, Bernkasteler Kurfürstlay	5,50
Rhein, Deidesheimer Hofstück	5,50
Badischer Spätburgunder Weißherbst	6,50
Edelzwicker	6,00

STUDENT A   STUDENT A   STUDENT A   STUDENT A   STUDENT A

Television programmes   A11

You are looking forward to watching television; when you turn to the programme page in your newspaper, however, you discover that a member of your family has cut something out from the other side and left holes in the programme details. Ring your friend and ask him/her to provide all the missing details. Make a note of the programmes and times.

SONNTAG

I. Programm (ARD)

- 9.30 Programmvorschau
- 10.00 Mein Tagebuch (3)
- 10.45 Die Sendung mit der Maus
- 11.15 Kaffee oder Tee?
- 12.00 Der Internationale Frühschoppen
- 12.45 ...
- 13.15 Ludwig van Beethoven: Sonate für Klavier C-Dur op. 53 „Waldsteinsonate"
- 13.45 Magazin der Woche Regionalumschau
- 14.30 Besuch bei den Besuchern
- 15.00 Die große Chance (Siehe Vorschau)
- 16.35 Der alte Dämon
- 17.00 Glaubensinformation: Hoffnung
- 17.30 ARD-Ratgeber: Reise
- 18.15 Wir über uns Fernsehen in eigener Sache
- 18.20 Tagesschau
- ... Putsch; Versöhnung im Libanon; Die dreckigen Geschäfte der Milizen, Finanzierung der IRA und UDA in Irland; Norwegen und die Deutschen; Gesund in China
- 20.00 Tagesschau
- 20.15 Duell ohne Gnade (Siehe Vorschau)
- ... 100 Meisterwerke G. Bellini: Gebet Christi im Garten Gethsemane
- ... Tagesschau
- ... Erlöst oder betrogen? (Siehe Vorschau)
- ... ARD-Sport extra Golf-Masters-Turnier in Augusta (USA)
- ... Tagesschau

II. Programm

- 10.00 Programmvorschau
- 10.30 ZDF-Matinee u.a. Die Balance der Biosphäre (Wh)
- 12.00 Das Sonntagskonzert Gast: Dagmar Koller
- 12.45 Freizeit ... und was man daraus machen kann
- 13.15 Chronik der Woche Reichere Bürger – ärmerer Staat?
- 13.40 Kreta – Ursprung Europas (1)
- 14.10 Löwenzahn
- 14.40 ...
- 14.45 Danke schön Die Aktion Sorgenkind berichtet
- 14.50 Das große Abenteuer (sw) (Siehe Vorschau)
- 16.15 Götzendämmerung Notizen zu Thomas Manns „Zauberberg"
- 17.00 Heute
- 17.02 Die Sport-Reportage u.a. Eishockeymeisterschaft: Play-Off-Spiel Landshut – Köln; 2. Fußball-Bundesliga
- 18.00 Tagebuch Aktuelles aus der katholischen Kirche
- 18.15 Liebt diese Erde (3)
- 18.58 Programmvorschau
- 19.00 Heute
- 19.10 Bonner Perspektiven Koalitionsstreit: Ausländerpolitik
- 19.30 Erkennen Sie die Melodie?
- 20.15 ...
- 22.05 ...
- 22.20 ...
- 23.05 ...
- 0.05 ...

- 9.00 ...
- 9.25 ...
- 9.55 Betriebswirtschaftslehre und Rechnungswesen
- 10.25 Biologie
- 15.30 Schach für jedermann
- 15.45 Das internationale TV-Kochbuch
- 16.00 Sehen statt hören Ein Wochenmagazin für
- 17.30 ...
- 18.00 ...
- 18.30 ...
- 19.00 ...
- 20.00 ...
- 23.20 Nachgespielt Das Verhalten der Tiere (5)
- 0.05 Nachrichten

STUDENT A   **STUDENT A**   **STUDENT A**   **STUDENT A**   **STUDENT A**

A12 A hotel questionnaire

You work for the Hotel Ziegler in Hamburg. The Hotel is currently conducting a survey to discover how satisfied guests have been with what it has to offer. You put questions to guests as they are departing. Your partner will play the part of Herr/Frau Kaufmann: ask him/her the questions which will enable you to complete the Hotel's questionnaire.

Fragebogen

Name des Hotelgasts: _____

Geschlecht: männlich ☐   Alter ☐
            weiblich ☐

Wohnort: _____

Dauer des Aufenthalts _____ Tage

Zweck des Aufenthalts   Urlaub ☐
(bitte ankreuzen)   Geschäftsreise ☐
                       Privatbesuch ☐
                       Sonstiges ☐

Waren Sie im allgemeinen mit Ihrem Zimmer zufrieden?
  ja ☐
  nein ☐

Wie hat Ihnen folgendes gefallen?

	nicht gut	gut	sehr gut
Anlage des Hotels			
Einrichtung des Zimmers			
Restaurant			
Frühstück			
Bedienung			

Haben Sie das Telefon benutzt?
  ja ☐
  nein ☐

Wir danken Ihnen für Ihre Hilfe!

STUDENT A

A penfriend's letter — A13

Your German penfriend has written you a letter suggesting that you might meet when she is in England. Unfortunately your dog chewed up the letter before you could get to it and some vital information is missing. You ring your penfriend and ask her for the missing details.

Liebe Becky,

Es tut mir wirklich leid, daß ich nicht schon längst geschrieben habe, aber leider wurde mein sehr krank, und wir hatten so viel zu tun. Aber jetzt ist alles wieder in Ordnung, und ich habe eine große Überraschung für Dich! Unser Schulorchester fährt nach England und ich darf mitfahren, obgleich ich kein Instrument spiele! Ist das nicht einfach toll! Wir fahren am und, wenn alles klappt, sind wir am in unserem Hotel, ganz in der Nähe von Meine Frage ist: Könnten wir uns treffen? Am Tage nach unserer Ankunft in könnte ich allein mit dem fahren, und Dich dann in treffen. Was hältst Du davon?

Laß mich bitte sofort wissen, ob wir uns treffen können!

Bis bald!

Deine
Steffi

STUDENT A   STUDENT A   STUDENT A   STUDENT A   STUDENT A

A14 Planning your flights

You are in Germany and decide that it will be useful while there to plan your next trip. You will need to fly to Hannover on Thursday 12 September, to travel from there by air on the following day to Stuttgart, and to return to Heathrow on Saturday 21 September. You will need to be in Hannover by 5 pm at the latest and in Stuttgart the next day by 2 pm. You will want to do some shopping on your last day in Germany and so would like to return to Heathrow late, if that is possible. Ring a local travel agent and ask about appropriate flights. Ask for times, flight numbers, flight duration and airline. Record the flights you decide on; some flights will already be fully booked.

Datum	Ziel	Flugnummer	Zeit	Fluglinie

STUDENT A   STUDENT A   STUDENT A   STUDENT A   STUDENT A

Writing a school report

A15

You are Herr Heinemann, a teacher at the Albrecht-Dürer-Schule in Cologne; your headmaster has asked you to rewrite a school report since some ink was spilt on it in the school office. When you sit down at home to fill in a new report form you discover that you have left the original at school. You can remember some of the details, but have to ring the headmaster, Herr Schneider, to fill in the rest.

Albrecht-Dürer-Schule
(Name der Schule)

Brigitte
Klasse........   Schuljahr 19 85/6....   1. Halbjahr

Verhalten: gut
Mitarbeit: befriedigend

Leistungen in den Einzelfächern

Religionslehre	sehr gut	Bildhaftes Gestalten	gut
Deutsch		Werken	—
Geschichte		Handarbeit	
Gemeinschaftskunde	ausreichend	Hauswerk	—
Erdkunde	gut		—
Englisch/Französisch		Arbeitsgemeinschaften	
Mathematik		Französisch/Englisch	—
Physik	ausreichend	Kurzschrift	
Chemie		Maschinenschreiben	sehr gut
Biologie	gut		
Leibesübungen			
Musik	gut		

Bemerkungen:
....
....

........Köln........, den 3. März 19 86

Klassenlehrer: Dienststempel   Schulleiter:

Heinemann

Unterschrift eines Erziehungsberechtigten: ....

STUDENT A   STUDENT A   STUDENT A   STUDENT A   STUDENT A

A16 Aunt Hildegard's letter

You have been expecting a letter from your Aunt Hildegard who has threatened to come to stay with you for a day or so. Ring home to ask your wife/husband if the letter has arrived yet. You are hoping that Aunt Hildegard will only want to stay for two nights and that she will come by train and taxi, so that you do not have to fetch her. You hope too that she will spend one evening away from the house with her friend who lives nearby, and that she will leave her dog Mitzi at home this time.

Ask your wife/husband:

- (a) if the letter has come;
- (b) when your aunt is going to arrive;
- (c) how she is intending to travel;
- (d) how long she will be staying;
- (e) if she is leaving her dog at home;
- (f) if she plans to do anything else while she is with you.

Your wife/husband will provide appropriate responses.

STUDENT A   STUDENT A   STUDENT A   STUDENT A   STUDENT A

Completing a telegram   A17

Your employer is staying at a hotel in Berlin. During his absence an important invitation has arrived for him. You ring him and he asks you for the details. Since it seems impossible for him to attend, you suggest that he should send a telegram declining the invitation. Here is the text of the invitation:

> Sehr geehrter Herr Schäfer,
>
> wir bitten Sie, an einer Tagung über das Thema 'Aktuelle Probleme im Wirtschaftsleben' teilzunehmen. Die Tagung wird in der Zeit vom 15.9 (Anreise) bis 19.9 (Abreise) im Hotel zu Vier Jahreszeiten in Wien stattfinden. Wir hoffen sehr auf Ihre Mitarbeit an dieser Tagung!
>
> Mit freundlichen Grüßen,
> Dr Martin Körner

STUDENT A

A18 Laundry and dry-cleaning

You and your wife/husband are on holiday in Munich and have accumulated a lot of washing. The list below indicates which items of clothing you need to have washed, pressed, or dry-cleaned. Your partner will play the assistant in a laundry/dry cleaner's. Tell him/her which items you have. He/she will then make a list. Ask how much each item will cost and what the total will be.

Stückzahl	Damen-Wäsche
2	Blusen
1	Nachthemden
	Schlafanzüge
	Unterhemden
	Unterkleider
4	Schlupfhosen
3	Büstenhalter
3	Taschentücher
3	Paar Strümpfe
	Herren-Wäsche
4	Oberhemden
	Smokinghemden
	Nachthemden
1	Schlafanzüge
4	Unterhosen
	Unterhemden
4	Paar Socken
2	Taschentücher

Stückzahl	Reinigung	Bügeldienst	Damen
1	✓		Kleid
			Abendkleid
			Kostüm
			Jacke
1	✓		Rock
			Hose
			Mantel (leicht)
			Mantel (schwer)
			Pullover
			Bluse
1		✓	Faltenrock ab 6 Falten
			Schal

Stückzahl	Reinigung	Bügeldienst	Herren
			Anzug
1	✓		Jacke
			Weste
2	✓		Hose
			Trenchcoat
			Smoking
			Mantel (leicht)
			Mantel (schwer)
			Krawatte
			Schal
			Pullover
			Hemd
1		✓	Hemd handgebügelt

STUDENT A   STUDENT A   STUDENT A   STUDENT A   STUDENT A

A trip to Bonn

A19

You are away from home on a trip to Bonn. You ring your wife to say that you will be arriving home at about 8 pm. She asks you questions about how you have spent your time in Bonn and elsewhere. Reconstruct your day from the items below.

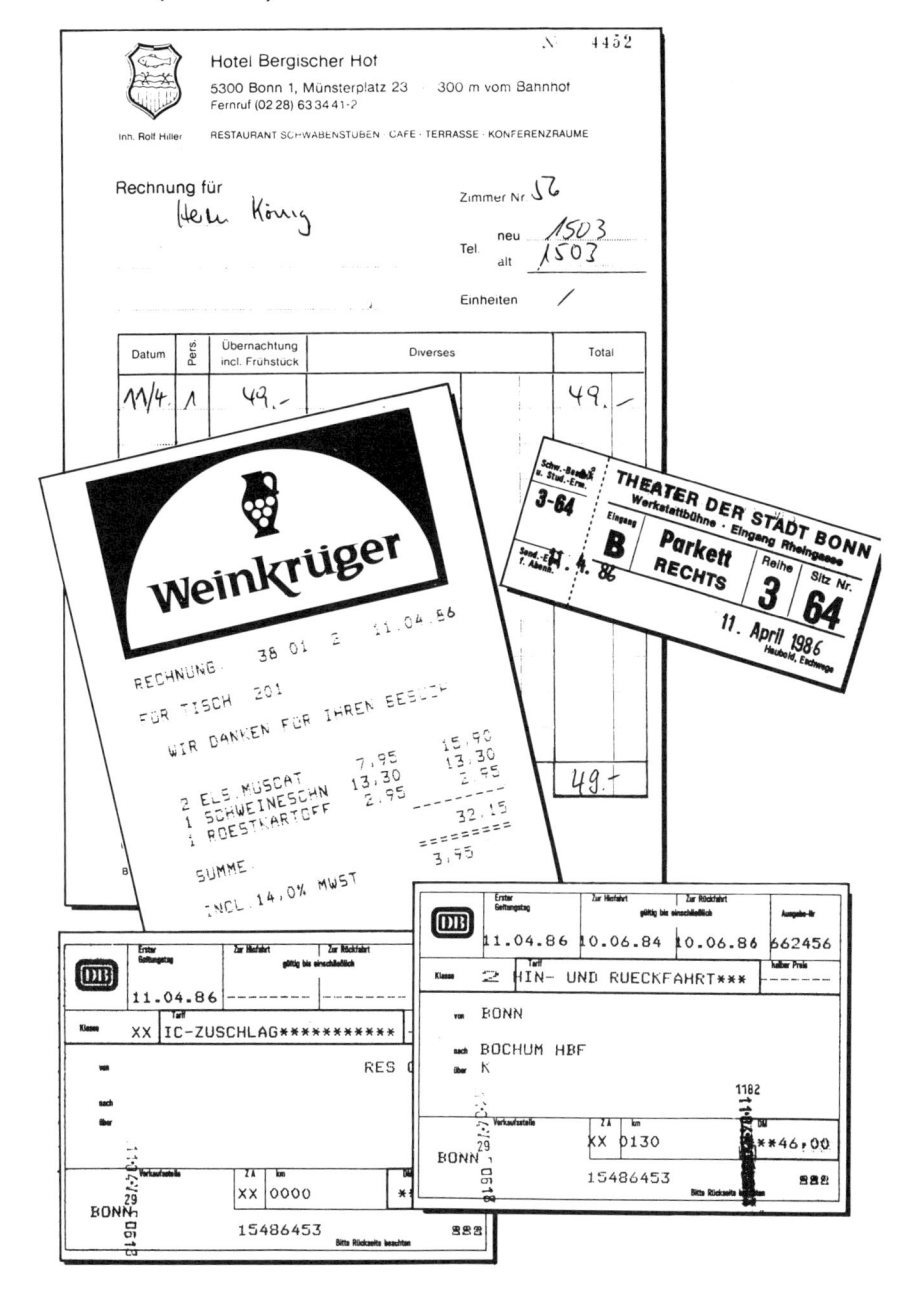

STUDENT A   STUDENT A   STUDENT A   STUDENT A   STUDENT A

A20 Eating out in Berlin

You are interested in meeting your friend at a good specialist restaurant in Berlin. Ring and ask the questions below. Record the information you are given and then tell your friend which restaurant you have chosen and when you would like to meet.

How many Chinese restaurants would your friend recommend?
At what times are they open?
How many Greek restaurants are possible?
Are there any Greek restaurants in the Joachimstaler Straße?
What are their names and opening times?
Is there a restaurant which specialises in cheese dishes?
Is it open on a Monday?
What other specialist restaurants are there?
Is there anywhere which allows you to eat outside?

Having received this information you decide that a French restaurant would be best. Ask for:

(a) its name;
(b) its address;
(c) its telephone number;
(d) its opening times.

Say that you will meet your friend there at 8.30 pm.

STUDENT A   STUDENT A   STUDENT A   STUDENT A   STUDENT A

At a camp-site in Germany

A21

You are the owner of a camp-site in Germany. A German family is just departing after a few days' holiday at the camp. Ask them questions which will allow you to complete their bill. You will need to know:

(a) their name;
(b) their address;
(c) their nationality;
(d) how many children;
(e) how many adults;
(f) whether they have a car;
(g) whether they have a tent or a caravan;
(h) how many nights they stayed.

Here is the tariff:

Erwachsene	(pro Nacht)	. . .	DM 4,-
Kinder	(pro Nacht)	. . .	DM 3,-
Auto	(pro Nacht)	. . .	DM 3,50
Zelt	(pro Nacht)	. . .	DM 3,50
Wohnwagen	(pro Nacht)	. . .	DM 8,-

Camping Sonnenberg	
Name:	
Adresse:	
Staatsangehörigkeit:	
	DM
. . . . Erwachsene	
. . . . Kinder	
. . . . Auto(s)	
. . . . Zelt(e)	
. . . . Wohnwagen	
Zwischensumme:	
. . . . x Nächte @	
Gesamtsumme:	

STUDENT A STUDENT A STUDENT A STUDENT A STUDENT A

A22 Breakfast in the Kempinski

You are responsible for room service on a floor of the famous Kempinski Hotel in Berlin. Two of the guests on your floor have hung lists on their doors indicating what kind of breakfast they would like delivered to their room. Ring down to your colleague in the kitchen and make the necessary arrangements.

Form 1:

Anzahl der Gäste: 2   Zimmer-Nummer: 72
Name: RICHTER

BRISTOL HOTEL Kempinski Berlin

Mein Frühstück um:/My breakfast at: 8³⁰–9⁰⁰ ✓

Einfaches Frühstück mit:/Continental Breakfast with:
- Kaffee ✓
- Tee ✓
- Schokolade ✓
- Milch: kalt ✓, Zitrone/lemon

Säfte/Juice:
- Orange ✓
- Tomate ✓

- natur ✓
- Joghurt ✓

Eierspeisen/Egg Dishes:
- 2 Spiegeleier ✓

Aufschnitt/Cold Cuts:
- Gemischter Aufschnitt ✓

Gesamtsumme: 18257

Besondere Wünsche/Special requests – Tageszeitung/Newspaper: FRANKFURTER ALLGEMEINE

Form 2:

Anzahl der Gäste: 1   Zimmer-Nummer: 67
Name: Dr. KÖRNER

BRISTOL HOTEL Kempinski Berlin

Mein Frühstück um:/My breakfast at: 7³⁰–8⁰⁰ ✓

Einfaches Frühstück mit:/Continental Breakfast with:
- Kaffee ✓
- Milch: kalt ✓

Säfte/Juice:
- Grapefruit ✓

- Grapefruit ½
- Joghurt

Eierspeisen/Egg Dishes:
- 1 gekochtes Ei ✓
- Würstchen ✓

Aufschnitt/Cold Cuts:
- Käse nach Wahl ✓

Gesamtsumme: 16441

Besondere Wünsche/Special requests – Tageszeitung/Newspaper: Die Welt

STUDENT A STUDENT A STUDENT A STUDENT A STUDENT A

Arranging a business appointment — A23

You are Frau Richter, a busy sales director of a local firm. Ring your business associate Herr Naumann and try to fix a time at which you can both meet. You will need two hours for the meeting. He will suggest times too. If they are not possible, explain why. What time do you both decide on?

Februar/März	
27 So	11.00 Kirche 14.00 zu Tante Erika (+ Abendessen)
28 Mo	9.00–12.00 Konferenz 14.00 → Berlin
01 Di	Berlin (abends zurück)
02 Mi	14.00–18.00 Messe
03 Do	9.00–10.00 Verabredung: Herr Müller 14.00–14.30 Zahnarzt
04 Fr	20.00 Party b. Schmidts
05 Sa	Urlaub beginnt

STUDENT A   STUDENT A   STUDENT A   STUDENT A   STUDENT A

A24 Sightseeing in Berlin

You are in a telephone box in Berlin at the corner of Bismarckstraße and Leibnizstraße. You ring the bus company Berolina to ask about their sightseeing tours of Berlin. Ask which tours will show you the following places of interest and find out at which time(s) each tour leaves; ask too how long each tour lasts and how much it costs.

	Tour No.	Time(s)	Duration	Cost
Night life in the city				
Historic sights				
Potsdam (half day)				

Ask too how to get to the starting-point for the tours.

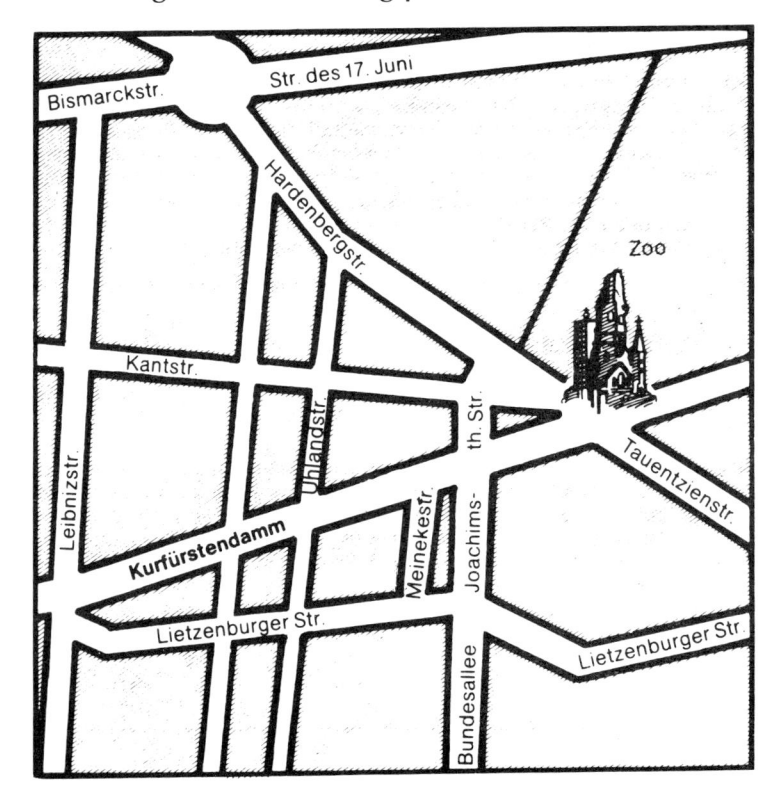

STUDENT A   STUDENT A   STUDENT A   STUDENT A   STUDENT A

House-hunting

A25

You are house-hunting with your wife/husband and have only time to visit properties separately. You then ring each other to describe the houses you have looked at. Here is a plan of the house you have been viewing. Ring your wife/husband and describe it in detail. He/she will make a quick sketch from your description which you can compare later.

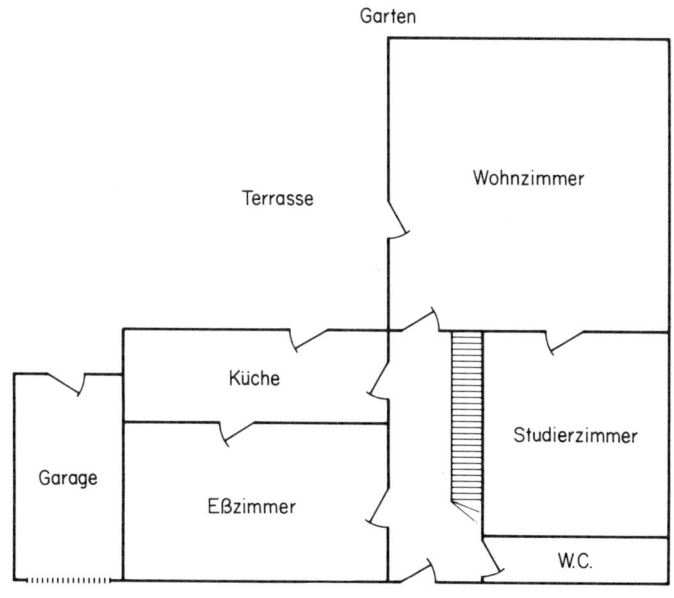

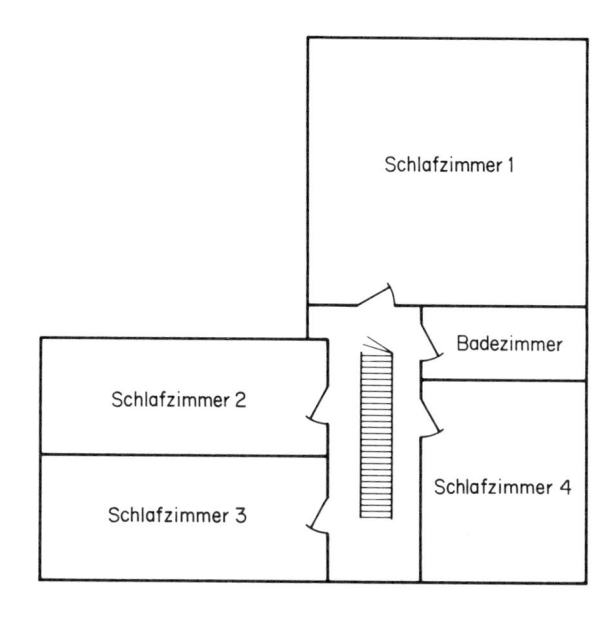

Garten

Terrasse

Wohnzimmer

Küche

Studierzimmer

Garage

Eßzimmer

W.C.

Schlafzimmer 1

Badezimmer

Schlafzimmer 2

Schlafzimmer 4

Schlafzimmer 3

STUDENT A   STUDENT A   STUDENT A   STUDENT A   STUDENT A

A26 Theatre-going

You wish to plan some visits to theatres in Berlin during the first half of July. Ring the ticket agency and ask for the following information:

(a) What is the address and telephone number of the Freie Volksbühne?
(b) What is on at the Renaissance-Theater on 16 July?
(c) At what time does the performance of 'Stella' begin on 2 July at the Schloßpark-Theater?
(d) At what theatre is there a performance of 'Amadeus'? When? At what time? What is the address and telephone number of the theatre?
(e) What opera is being performed on Saturday 7 July?
(f) Is 'Simon Boccanegra' being sung in German?
(g) When is the first night of 'Ritt auf die Wartburg'?
(h) When do the *Theaterferien* begin at the Deutsche Oper?

Your partner will provide appropriate answers. Make a note of them.

STUDENT A STUDENT A STUDENT A STUDENT A STUDENT A

Planning a train journey — A27

1. You are at the information office in the railway station in Kiel and wish to find out the following information:

   – which trains leave Kiel for Düsseldorf between 9.00 and 11.30 am, and when do they arrive there?

   – which InterCity train would you need to get to arrive in Düsseldorf between 9.00 and 12.30 am, and when does it arrive there?

   – what connections are there from Essen to Kiel between midday and 5.00 pm?

   Ask the clerk appropriate questions and record the information below:

2. You are a clerk in the information office at the railway station in Kiel. A traveller asks you about the times of various trains. Provide the information from your copy of the timetable below:

A28 Making a *Sachertorte*

You have been trying to bake a Viennese chocolate cake, a *Sachertorte*, but it has been a disaster, mainly, you think, because you were following the recipe from memory. You used:

    8 eggs
    130 g butter
    100 g sugar
    100 g flour
    150 g chocolate
strawberry jam

You tried to bake it fairly quickly, in a hot oven. Ring your friend, who you know has successfully baked *Sachertorten* before, and check where your ingredients and method of preparation went wrong.

STUDENT A   STUDENT A   STUDENT A   STUDENT A   STUDENT A

A trip to Munich

A29

You are a teacher organising a trip to Munich for a group of your pupils. You do not know the city, and so you ring a colleague in Munich and ask him/her to describe to you the main places of interest. Identify their position on the map below and record basic information about each of them.

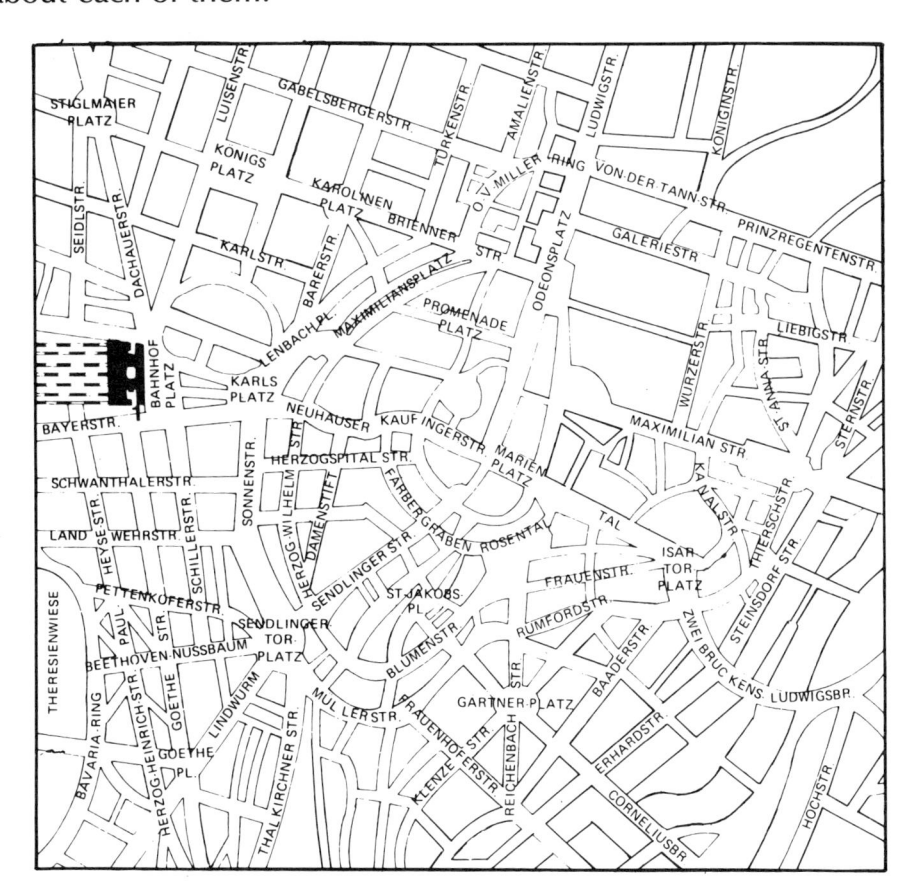

1.
2.
3.
4.
5.
6.
7.
8.
9.
10.

STUDENT A   STUDENT A   STUDENT A   STUDENT A   STUDENT A

A30 Registering a change of address

You have just moved house from Munich to the small town of Ludwigshausen in southern Bavaria. You have to register your new address and full details of your family with the local authorities. You visit the town hall for this purpose, and an official there fills in the appropriate form for you. The information you will need to give him is as follows: your name is Heinrich Josef Herzberg; your wife, Hildegard Agnes (née Sigl) is Austrian; you have three children (Peter, born 8.1.73, Karl-Heinz, born 9.2.75, Jutta Maria, born 11.6.78); you were born on 8.11.50 and your wife on 9.10.51; you are a post office worker and your wife is a teacher; your previous address was Kirchenstraße 153, 8000 München; you moved to your new address five days ago.

STUDENT B   STUDENT B   STUDENT B   STUDENT B   STUDENT B

Looking for a hotel

B1

You work in the Information office in Bonn. A visitor rings from the main station to ask about the availability of hotel rooms with showers for the next two nights. According to your information there are only three hotels left with such a vacancy. They are the Bergischer Hof (in the Münsterplatz, marked A on your map), the Löhndorf (in the Stockenstraße, marked B) and the Muskewitz (in the Dechenstraße, marked C). Explain to the tourist how to get to each of these hotels from the main station.

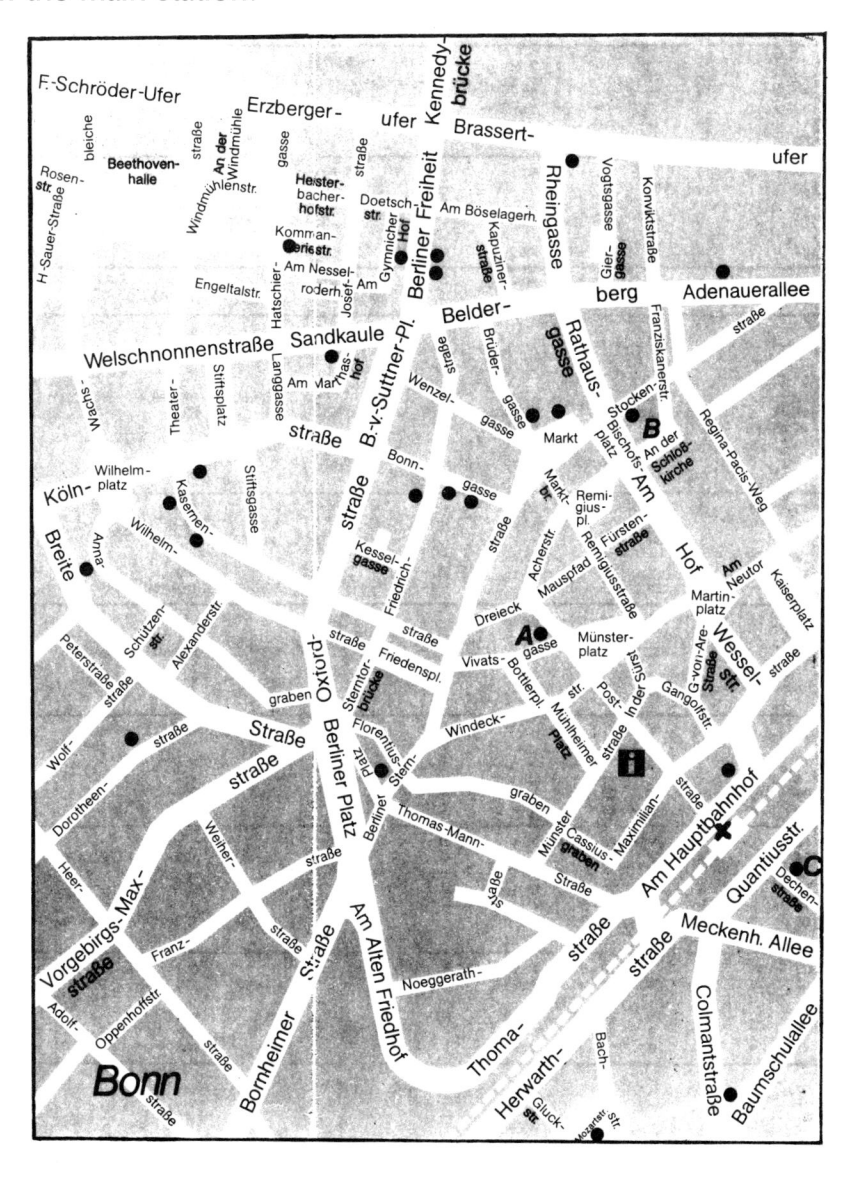

STUDENT B   STUDENT B   STUDENT B   STUDENT B   STUDENT B

B2 A robbery witnessed

You are a policeman investigating a robbery that has just taken place at a jeweller's shop in Frankfurt. A witness has come forward who saw someone driving away from the scene of the crime. Ask questions as follows:

(a) at what time did the robbery happen?
(b) what did the person look like?
(c) what was he wearing?
(d) was he carrying anything?
(e) what sort of car was he driving?
(f) did you get the registration number?
(g) did anyone else see what happened?

STUDENT B   STUDENT B   STUDENT B   STUDENT B   STUDENT B

Hunt-the-thimble

B3

Below is a sketch of a sitting room. Play a version of 'Hunt-the-thimble' with your partner. You decide where to hide a small object in the room and your partner has to guess where and what it is. Your partner begins, then you take it turns.

STUDENT B   STUDENT B   STUDENT B   STUDENT B   STUDENT B

B4 A guessing game

Your partner will choose one of the people pictured below and you must ask questions to enable you to guess which face has been chosen.

When you have guessed the correct face it will be your turn to choose somebody and your partner must then guess which face you have chosen.

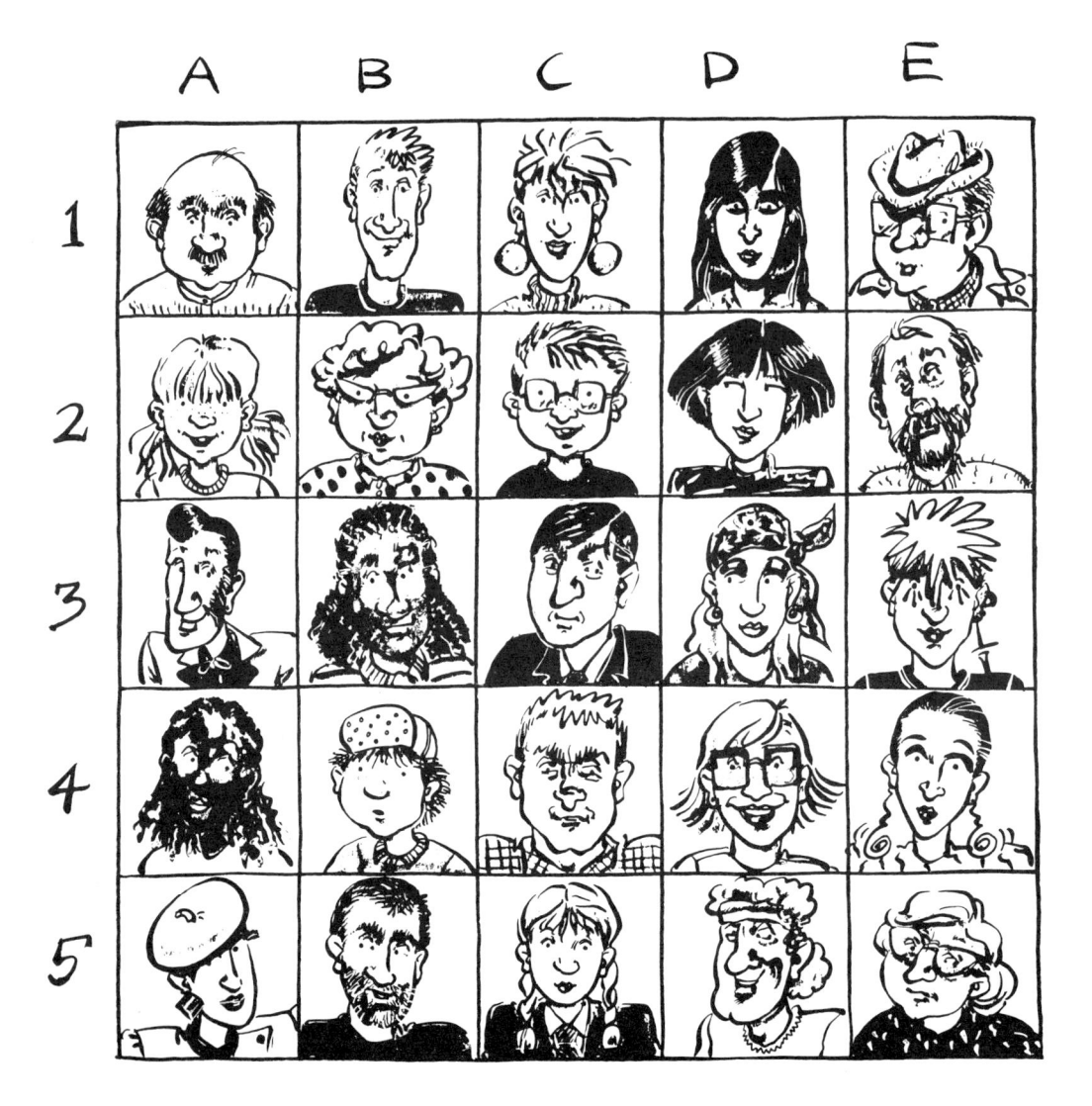

STUDENT B

A spoilt menu   B5

You and your friend are in a restaurant in Düsseldorf. You decide to choose something form the chef's special menu, but unfortunately previous diners have spilt coffee over your copy, obscuring some of the details. Ask your friend to supply the missing information. Your friend has similar problems; he/she will begin.

```
▀▀▀▀▀▀▀▀▀▀▀▀ ZUM GOLDENEN OCHSEN ▀▀▀▀▀▀▀▀▀▀▀▀

                    Unser
                    Küchenchef
                    empfiehlt:


        200   Putenbruststeak "Indische Art"
              mit geb. Früchten, Butterreis
              und grünem Salat             DM  19,75

        201   Hamburger Krustentiersuppe
              mit Sahnehaube                            DM   6,25

              V O R S P E I S E N

        202   Matjesröllchen "Lord - Nelson" auf Apfelring, gefüllt mit
              Sahnemeerrettich und Preiselbeeren, dazu Vollkornbrot und Butter   DM  11,50

        203   Tatar vom Silberlachs mit pochiertem Ei,
              Kräutermeerrettich, Toast und Butter      DM  15,25

        204   Toast "Wellington" klei███████████
              mit Roquefortbirne█                       DM  18,00

              H A U P T G E R I C H T E

        205   Rinderleber "Berliner Art" mit Röstzwiebeln, Apfelringen,
              dazu Kartoffelmus und gemischter Salat    DM █████

        206   "Osso███████inscheiben mit Tomaten
              ges██████ghetti, dazu grüner Salat        DM  20,25

        207   █████████"Kaukasische Art"
              ██████üse und Pommes frites               DM  23,50

        208   Kalbsnierenscheiben in Dijonersenfcreme
              auf Blattspinat und Sahnekartoffeln       DM  24,50

        209   Rumpsteak "Westmoreland"
              mit ███ggemüse und Röstkartoffeln         DM  24,50

        210   ████n in Dillrahmsauce
              ████tterkartoffeln und Gurkensalat        DM  22,75

        211   Ochsenlendenstück in Schneckensauce
              mit Zucchinischeiben und Schneekartoffeln DM  28,75

              D E S S E R T

        212   Crêpes mit Grand Marnier und Vanilleeis   DM   8,75
```

In obigen Preisen sind Bedienung und gesetzl. MwSt. enthalten.

STUDENT B   STUDENT B   STUDENT B   STUDENT B   STUDENT B

B6 The ideal timetable

You are a pupil being interviewed by a reporter from the local radio station who is working on a programme on pupils' attitudes to school. You will be asked what your ideal school timetable would look like. Fill in the blank timetable below, deciding on times of lessons, length of break, times at which school would begin and end each day, and what subjects would be studied. When you have filled in the details the reporter will ask you for full details and enter them on his/her copy of the blank timetable.

STUNDENPLAN Klasse_____ Sommer/Winter-Halbjahr 19____

ZEIT	MONTAG	DIENSTAG	MITTWOCH	DONNERSTAG	FREITAG	SONNABEND

Now turn the tables on your interviewer and ask him/her to decide on an ideal timetable. Ask questions that will enable you to enter full details of the timetable on the blank below.

STUNDENPLAN Klasse_____ Sommer/Winter-Halbjahr 19____

ZEIT	MONTAG	DIENSTAG	MITTWOCH	DONNERSTAG	FREITAG	SONNABEND

STUDENT B   STUDENT B   STUDENT B   STUDENT B   STUDENT B

The Berlin Underground — B7

You approach an information desk in the Berlin Underground in order to ask how to travel between various stations in the network. You will be told at which stations you must change in each case. Make a note of the details and then check them back.

You want to know how to get from:

Uhlandstraße	to	Innsbrucker Platz
Tegel	to	Anhalter Bahnhof
Deutsche Oper	to	Kurfürstenstraße
Nollendorfplatz	to	Friedrichstraße
Charlottenburg	to	Krumme Lanke

Anfang	Umsteigebahnhof (-höfe)	Ziel
Uhlandstraße		Innsbrucker Platz
Tegel		Anhalter Bahnhof
Deutsche Oper		Kurfürstenstraße
Nollendorfplatz		Friedrichstraße
Charlottenburg		Krumme Lanke

STUDENT B   STUDENT B   STUDENT B   STUDENT B   STUDENT B

B8 A burgled flat

You are Herr/Frau Kellermann, enjoying a holiday on the Baltic coast. Your neighbour, who has been looking after your flat while you are away, rings to say that there has been a burglary and several items appear to be missing. You are asked to describe exactly what was in your sitting room. Your neighbour will tell you whether each item is still there or not. Make a list of the missing items.

STUDENT B   STUDENT B   STUDENT B   STUDENT B   STUDENT B

Choosing a holiday

B9

You are an employee of a travel agency. A client will ask you about various possibilities for a short holiday. Describe the holidays outlined below and help your client towards a decision. Confirm the details of the holiday he/she eventually decides on.

15 TAGE
SONNE! MEER!
IBIZA
MODERNES HOTEL
incl. Flug
DM 2000,–
(Ab 1. August)

PARIS
10 Tage
SONDERANGEBOT!
DM 600,–
Juni – September

ROM
Nur DM 400,–!
5 TAGE
Kleines Hotel
(incl. Frühstück!)

7 TAGE
LONDON
traditionelles Hotel im Stadtzentrum
DM 500,–
(incl. Frühstück)

DONAUFAHRT
Linz – Wien und Zurück
5 TAGE
Juni / Juli
Inclusivpreis
DM 550,–

STUDENT B   STUDENT B   STUDENT B   STUDENT B   STUDENT B

B10 Ordering drinks

You are a waiter/waitress in a bar-restaurant. A party of 13 has arrived, and you take their orders from the *Getränkekarte*. Note down on your pad what they order, and tell the leader of the party the amount due. He/she will query it and check individual prices with you.

Biere vom Faß		
Schultheiß Pilsener	0,2 l	2,10
Schultheiß Pilsener	0,4 l	4,20
König Pilsener	0,2 l	2,50
König Pilsener	0,4 l	5,00
Flaschenbiere		
Schultheiß Pilsener	0,33 l	4,10
Schultheiß Malz	0,33 l	3,50
Weizenbier	0,50 l	5,50
Diät Pils	0,33 l	4,50
Erfrischungen		
Tonic-Water Schweppes	Fl. 0,2 l	3,75
Bitter-Lemon	Fl. 0,2 l	3,75
Coca-Cola	Fl. 0,2 l	3,25
Fanta Orange	Fl. 0,2 l	3,25
Apfelsaft	Fl. 0,2 l	3,75
Orangensaft	Fl. 0,2 l	4,00
Tomatensaft	Fl. 0,2 l	4,00
Warme Getränke		
Tasse Kaffee		2,25
Kännchen Kaffee		4,50
Glas Tee		2,25
Kännchen Tee		4,50
Tasse Schokolade		2,50
Glas Glühwein		5,50
Glas Grog von 4 cl Rum		7,00
Schoppenweine (0,2 l)		
Mosel, Bernkasteler Kurfürstlay		5,50
Rhein, Deidesheimer Hofstück		5,50
Badischer Spätburgunder Weißherbst		6,50
Edelzwicker		6,00

STUDENT B   STUDENT B   STUDENT B   STUDENT B   STUDENT B

Television programmes

B11

Your friend, who has been looking forward to watching television, rings to say that a member of his/her family has cut pieces out of the newspaper and there are holes in the programme page. You are asked to provide all the missing details from your complete copy.

SONNTAG

I. Programm (ARD)

- 9.30 Programmvorschau
- 10.00 Mein Tagebuch (3)
- 10.45 Die Sendung mit der Maus
- 11.15 Kaffee oder Tee?
- 12.00 Der Internationale Frühschoppen
  Wieder Krieg in Vietnam?
  Teilnehmer: James Markham, USA; Yuh-Huei Chen, China; Andreas Kohlschütter, Schweiz; Gerd Ruge, Deutschland, und Werner Höfer
- 12.45 Tagesschau
  Wochenspiegel
- 13.15 Emil Gilels spielt
  Ludwig van Beethoven:
  Sonate für Klavier C-Dur op. 53
  „Waldsteinsonate"
- 13.45 Magazin der Woche
  Regionalumschau
- 14.30 Besuch bei den Besuchern
- 15.00 Die große Chance
  (Siehe Vorschau)
- 16.35 Der alte Dämon
- 17.00 Glaubensinformation: Hoffnung
- 17.30 ARD-Ratgeber: Reise
- 18.15 Wir über uns
  Fernsehen in eigener Sache
- 18.20 Tagesschau
- 18.23 Die Sportschau
  u.a. Motorrad-Trial; Rad: Lüttich-Bastogne-Lüttich; Box-Bundesliga: Frankfurt-Leverkusen
- 19.20 Weltspiegel
  Guinea nach dem Putsch; Versöhnung im Libanon; Die dreckigen Geschäfte der Milizen, Finanzierung der IRA und UDA in Irland; Norwegen und die Deutschen; Gesund in China
- 20.00 Tagesschau
- 20.15 Duell ohne Gnade
  (Siehe Vorschau)
- 21.55 100 Meisterwerke
  G. Bellini: Gebet Christi im Garten Gethsemane
- 22.05 Tagesschau
- 22.10 Erlöst oder betrogen?
  (Siehe Vorschau)
- 22.55 ARD-Sport extra
  Golf-Masters-Turnier in Augusta (USA)
- 1.00 Tagesschau

II. Programm

- 10.00 Programmvorschau
- 10.30 ZDF-Matinee
  u.a. Die Balance der Biosphäre (Wh)
- 12.00 Das Sonntagskonzert
  Gast: Dagmar Koller
- 12.45 Freizeit
  ... und was man daraus machen kann
- 13.15 Chronik der Woche
  Reichere Bürger — ärmerer Staat?
- 13.40 Kreta — Ursprung Europas (1)
- 14.10 Löwenzahn
- 14.40 Heute
- 14.45 Danke schön
  Die Aktion Sorgenkind berichtet
- 14.50 Das große Abenteuer (sw)
  (Siehe Vorschau)
- 16.15 Götzendämmerung
  Notizen zu Thomas Manns „Zauberberg"
- 17.00 Heute
- 17.02 Die Sport-Reportage
  u.a. Eishockeymeisterschaft: Play-Off-Spiel Landshut — Köln; 2. Fußball-Bundesliga
- 18.00 Tagebuch
  Aktuelles aus der katholischen Kirche
- 18.15 Liebt diese Erde (3)
- 18.58 Programmvorschau
- 19.00 Heute
- 19.10 Bonner Perspektiven
  Koalitionsstreit: Ausländerpolitik
- 19.30 Erkennen Sie die Melodie?
- 20.15 Der Zauberberg (1)
  (Siehe Vorschau)
- 22.05 Heute
  Sport am Sonntag
- 22.20 James Last in Brighton
- 23.05 Zeugen des Jahrhunderts
- 0.05 Heute

III. Programm (WDR Westdeutsches Fernsehen)

- 9.00 Telekolleg aktuell
- 9.25 Telekolleg I
  Englisch
- 9.55 Betriebswirtschaftslehre und Rechnungswesen
- 10.25 Biologie
- 15.30 Schach für jedermann
- 15.45 Das internationale TV-Kochbuch
- 16.00 Sehen statt hören
  Ein Wochenmagazin für Hörgeschädigte
- 16.30 Ihre Heimat — unsere Heimat
  Für Gastarbeiter aus Portugal, Italien und der Türkei
- 17.30 Thirty Minutes
- 18.00 Pan Tau
- 18.30 Kultur-Geschichten (2)
- 19.00 Aktuelle Stunde
- 20.00 Tagesschau
- 20.15 Französische Maler des 19. Jahrhunderts:
  Eugène Delacroix
- 21.00 Wirtschaftsstudio
- 21.45 Modest Mussorgsky:
  Bilder einer Ausstellung
- 23.20 Nachgespielt
  Das Verhalten der Tiere (5)
- 0.05 Nachrichten

STUDENT B · STUDENT B · STUDENT B · STUDENT B · STUDENT B

B12 A hotel questionnaire

You are Herr/Frau Kaufmann (aged 28). You have been staying for three nights in the Hotel Ziegler in Hamburg while visiting a relative who lives nearby. You yourself live in Kiel. You stayed in Room 37 and were reasonably satisfied with it: it had a telephone, which you used several times, and was quite comfortable. The hotel was not situated in a very attractive area, but it did have an excellent restaurant. Breakfast was a bit disappointing (the bread was slightly stale, your egg was too hard, and the coffee was a bit cold). The staff were not over-friendly, but certainly not impolite.

As you leave the hotel one of the staff asks if you would be prepared to take part in a survey. You agree, and are then asked various questions about your stay. Answer them using the information above.

STUDENT B

A penfriend's letter

B13

You have written to your English penfriend to say that you will be travelling to England soon and to ask if it will be possible for you both to meet. Your penfriend rings to say that her dog has chewed your letter and so some vital information is missing. She will ask you some questions – you provide the missing details. Here is the text of your original letter:

Liebe Becky,

Es tut mir wirklich leid, daß ich nicht schon längst geschrieben habe, aber leider wurde mein Bruder sehr krank, und wir hatten so viel zu tun. Aber jetzt ist alles wieder in Ordnung, und ich habe eine große Überraschung für Dich! Unser Schulorchester fährt nach England und ich darf mitfahren, obgleich ich kein Instrument spiele! Ist das nicht einfach toll! Wir fahren am 11. Oktober und, wenn alles klappt, sind wir am 12. Oktober in unserem Hotel, ganz in der Nähe von Dir in Oxford. Meine Frage ist: könnten wir uns treffen?

Am Tage nach unserer Ankunft in Henley könnte ich allein mit dem Bus nach Oxford fahren, und Dich dann in Oxford treffen. Was hältst Du davon?

Laß mich bitte sofort wissen, ob wir uns treffen können!

Bis bald!

Deine
Steffi

STUDENT B   STUDENT B   STUDENT B   STUDENT B   STUDENT B

B14 Planning your flights

You work in a German travel agency and receive a telephone enquiry about various flight possibilities. Provide the appropriate information from the timetables below. Some flights are already fully booked.

Heathrow ▶ Hannover

3 Apr – 11 Apr	1025	1250	LH039	727	
25 Mär – 29 Sep	1040	1305	LH049	737	[ausgebucht]
3 Apr – 11 Apr	1130	1355	BA772	TRD	
30 Sep – 27 Okt	1140	1305	LH049	737	
25 Mär – 29 Sep	1355	1620	BA774	73S	
30 Sep – 27 Okt	1455	1620	BA774	73S	
25 Mär – 29 Sep	1715	1940	BA776	B11	
30 Sep – 27 Okt	1815	1940	BA776	B11	

Stuttgart ▶ Heathrow

26 Mär – 29 Sep	0720	0755	LH062	737	
1 Okt – 27 Okt	0720	0855	LH062	737	
25 Mär – 28 Sep	1655	1725	LH066	737	[ausgebucht]
30 Sep – 26 Okt	1655	1825	LH066	737	
25 Mär – 27 Okt	1935(c)	2010	BA761	73S	

Hannover ▶ Stuttgart

1 Jan – 31 Dez	0505	0920	LH051	737	[ausgebucht]
1 Jan – 31 Dez	1110	1245	LH052	737	
1 Jan – 31 Dez	1725	1340	LH053	737	

STUDENT B   STUDENT B   STUDENT B   STUDENT B   STUDENT B

Writing a school report   B15

You are Herr Schneider, the headmaster of the Albrecht-Dürer-Schule in Cologne; a teacher at the school, Herr Heinemann, is having to rewrite the school report of one of the pupils. He rings you to ask if you will let him have some details from your copy of the pupil's report. Here is the original, which had ink spilt on it in the school office:

Albrecht-Dürer-Schule

Brigitte Untermeyer (Name der Schule)

Klasse 7b   Schuljahr 19 85/6   1. Halbjahr

Verhalten: gut
Mitarbeit: befriedigend

Leistungen in den Einzelfächern

Religionslehre	sehr gut	Bildhaftes Gestalten	gut
Deutsch	gut	Werken	—
Geschichte	ausreichend	Handarbeit	gut
Gemeinschaftskunde	ausreichend	Hauswerk	—
Erdkunde	gut		—
Englisch/Französisch	mangelhaft	**Arbeitsgemeinschaften**	
Mathematik	ausreichend	Französisch/Englisch	—
Physik	ausreichend	Kurzschrift	befriedigend
Chemie	mangelhaft	Maschinenschreiben	[ink blot]
Biologie	gut		
Leibesübungen	sehr gut		
Musik	gut		

Bemerkungen:

Brigitte zeigt leider kein Interesse an Englisch und Chemie; in den anderen Fächern hat sie fleißig gearbeitet

Köln , den 3. März 1986.

Klassenlehrer: Dienststempel   Schulleiter:
Heinemann   Schneider

Unterschrift eines Erziehungsberechtigten:

STUDENT B   STUDENT B   STUDENT B   STUDENT B   STUDENT B

B16 Aunt Hildegard's letter

Your wife/husband rings to ask if a letter has arrived from Aunt Hildegard. Say that it has, and provide answers to some questions about the contents of the letter.

> München, 8. Mai
>
> Meine Lieben!
>
> Es tut mir leid, daß ich nicht schon längst geschrieben habe. Jetzt kann ich Euch aber Bescheid sagen, daß ich Euch besuchen komme. Ich habe vor, übermorgen (Donnerstag) nach Hamburg zu reisen – und zwar mit dem Flugzeug! Ihr könnt mich ohne Probleme vom Flughafen abholen. Ihr werdet hoffentlich nichts dagegen haben, wenn ich diesmal fünf Tage bei Euch bleibe, d.h. bis Dienstag. Meine Bekannte in Hamburg, Frau Schöffler, würde uns gerne am Freitagabend besuchen. Sie darf wohl bei Euch zu Abend essen? Mitzi bringe ich mit, denn das liebe Hündchen fühlt sich immer so einsam, wenn es nicht mitkommen darf. Ich freue mich sehr darauf, bald wieder bei Euch zu sein!
>
> Mit herzlichen Grüßen,
> Eure
> Tante Hildegard

STUDENT B   **STUDENT B**   **STUDENT B**   **STUDENT B**   **STUDENT B**

Completing a telegram — B17

You are Herr Schäfer, a businessman currently staying in room 24 of the Kronprinz-Hotel in Berlin. It is 9.30 am on Monday 9 September. Your secretary rings to say that you have received an invitation to travel to Vienna to attend a conference. You ask for the details (who is the invitation from? dates, theme, place). Your secretary suggests that you should send a telegram to say that unfortunately you cannot attend. Complete the hotel form appropriately.

KRONPRINZ HOTEL

Tag u. Uhrzeit der Abfassung

Absender: _____

Zimmer Nr. _____

An Fernschreibstelle | **Fernschreiben / Telegramm**   Nichtzutreffendes streichen

An

Unterschrift:

Bei Fortsetzung Rückseite verwenden

STUDENT B

B18 Laundry and dry-cleaning

You work in a laundry/dry-cleaner's in Munich. A customer arrives with various items of clothing to be washed, pressed or dry-cleaned. Ask what items are involved, check them off on your lists, and let the customer know how much each item will cost and what the total bill will be.

WÄSCHELISTE

Damen-Wäsche	Preis	Stückzahl	DM	Pf
Blusen	10,–			
Nachthemden	7,–			
Schlafanzüge	7,50			
Unterhemden	2,50			
Unterkleider	5,50			
Schlupfhosen	3,–			
Büstenhalter	3,–			
Taschentücher	1,50			
Paar Strümpfe	2,–			

Herren-Wäsche				
Oberhemden	7,–			
Smokinghemden	10,–			
Nachthemden	7,–			
Schlafanzüge	7,50			
Unterhosen	3,–			
Unterhemden	3,–			
Paar Socken	2,–			
Taschentücher	1,50			

Summe

Total incl. MwSt

REINIGUNG/BÜGELDIENST-LISTE

DAMEN	Preis Reinigen	Preis Bügeln	Stückzahl	Betrag
Kleid	15,00	10,00		
Abendkleid	26,00	20,00		
Kostüm	21,00	16,00		
Jacke	11,00	9,00		
Rock	10,00	7,00		
Hose	10,00	7,00		
Mantel (leicht)	18,00	10,00		
Mantel (schwer)	20,00	12,00		
Pullover	7,00	5,00		
Bluse	7,50	5,00		
Faltenrock ab 6 Falten	12,00	10,00		
Schal	8,00	4,00		

HERREN				
Anzug	21,00	16,00		
Jacket	11,00	9,00		
Weste	6,00	4,00		
Hose	10,00	7,00		
Trenchcoat	18,00	11,00		
Smoking	24,00	18,00		
Mantel (leicht)	18,00	10,00		
Mantel (schwer)	20,00	12,00		
Krawatte	4,50	3,00		
Schal	4,50	3,00		
Pullover	7,00	5,00		
Hemd	5,50	3,00		
Hemd handgebügelt	7,50	5,00		

Summe

Total incl. MwSt

STUDENT B   STUDENT B   STUDENT B   STUDENT B   STUDENT B

A trip to Bonn   B19

You are Frau König. Your husband has been away on a short trip to Bonn and rings to tell you at what time he will be arriving home. You ask him about his trip: where did he stay? how much did the room cost? did that include breakfast? did he manage to travel to see his friend? where does he live? how did he get there? was it an expensive trip? where did he eat in the evening? what did he have to eat? did he drink much? how much did that cost? what else did he do in the evening? Your husband will provide appropriate answers.

STUDENT B · **STUDENT B** · **STUDENT B** · **STUDENT B** · **STUDENT B**

B20 Eating out in Berlin

Your friend rings you to arrange to meet for a meal in a specialist restaurant of some kind in Berlin. You have some information about a few places you might consider. Answer your friend's questions and make a note of the restaurant decided on and the time at which you will meet.

ASIA China-Restaurant
Das gemütliche und preiswerte
im Herzen von Berlin, Fasanen-/Ecke Kantstr. (vis-à-vis Theater d. Westens)
Ku'Damm-Nähe
Tägl. 12–24 Uhr · Tel. 312 80 99

Pierre
Cafe, Frühstück, französische Küche
Mo-Fr 10.00-2.00 Uhr
Sa, So 17.00-2.00 Uhr
Schaperstraße 17
gegenüber der Freien Volksbühne
☎ 881 12 14

HASENSTALL
Auf in den HASENSTALL
Die gemütliche kleine Bar mit Biergarten
Mo-Fr 17-3 Uhr
Sonnabend ab 18 Uhr
Kurfürstendamm 34 in der Passage
1000 Berlin 15
Inh. Helga Sterek ☎ (030) 883 28 63

Coq d'or
Das französische Feinschmeckerrestaurant in Berlin
geöffnet von 12 bis 2 Uhr früh
1 Berlin 31 · Dahlmannstraße 20 · Tel. 323 30 93
(20 m vom Kurfürstendamm entfernt)

BOKA-Grill
Orig. Jugoslawische Spezialitäten
Budweiser
Fasanenstr. 73/40 m Kudamm
Telefon 8 81 38 86
Tägl. 11.30–24 Uhr
durchgehend warme Küche

EL GRECO
GRIECHISCHE SPEZIALITÄTEN
HOLZKOHLENGRILL
BOUZOUKI LIVE jeden Freitag + Samstag
Marburger Str. 15 (am Europa-Center)
von 11.00–? ☎ 211 46 96

China-Restaurant Kwok
Berlin 30, Kurfürstenstr. 79
Geöffnet von 12–24 Uhr
Telefon 2 62 58 98

KÄSE KISTE
Warme und kalte Speisen
Di. – Do. 17 – 0.30 Uhr
Fr. – So. 12 – 0.30 Uhr
im Europacenter (1. Etage)

KATSCHKÖL
Einmalig in Berlin
Afghanisch
Essen und Trinken
in Original-Atmosphäre
Krumme Ecke Pestalozzi Str.
Tel: 312 34 72

MONTENEGRO GRILL
direkt neben Charlottenburger Schloß
Jugoslawische Spezialitäten
Spandauer Damm 42
1000 Berlin 19 · Telefon 322 52 94

China-Restaurant KAM SHING
1 Min. vom Kurfürstendamm in CITY-PASSAGE
Knesebeckstr. 56–58/Ecke Lietzenburger Str.
Tel. 882 23 80 · täglich von 12–24 Uhr
preiswerte Gruppenarrangements!

Restaurant LISSOS
Mediterrane Spezialitätenküche
Täglich geöffnet von 16–02 Uhr
1000 Berlin 15 · Pfalzburger Str. 83
Telefon 893 57 02

TAVERNA PLAKA
GRIECHISCHE SPEZIALITÄTEN Inh.: N. Rousvanidis
Öffnungszeiten Mo-Fr 17.00–2.00 Uhr · Sa-So 12.00–2.00 Uhr
1 Berlin 15, Joachimstaler Str. 17 · Tel. 88 31 55 7
Treppenaufgang Tivoli neben dem Parkhaus

"SOKRATES"
Griechische Spezialitäten
geöffnet von 11.00 – 4.00 früh
Joachimstaler Straße 21
Ecke Lietzenburger Straße
Telefon 88 166 59

CHINA-RESTAURANT TAI-TUNG
Berlin 30, Budapester Straße 50
Tägl. 12–24 Uhr · Tel. 2 61 30 91

STUDENT B   STUDENT B   STUDENT B   STUDENT B   STUDENT B

At a camp-site in Germany   B21

You are just leaving the 'Sonnenberg' camp-site after a few nights' stay. The owner is completing your bill and asks you some questions. Supply the appropriate answers and then ask him what the bill comes to.

You are a German family, consisting of yourself, your wife/husband, and three children; you live in Bad Godesberg (5300 Bonn-Bad Godesberg) in the Koblenzstraße (number 23); you stayed for four nights and you had with you one car, a caravan, and one tent for your son.

STUDENT B   STUDENT B   STUDENT B   STUDENT B   STUDENT B

B22 Breakfast at the Kempinski

You are working in the kitchens of the famous Kempinski Hotel in Berlin. Your colleague on one of the floors has to order breakfast for two guests requiring room service. Record their orders on your check-list.

Form 1

Anzahl der Gäste _____   Zimmer-Nummer _____
Name

BRISTOL HOTEL Kempinski Berlin

Mein Frühstuck um:/My breakfast at: am Pool gewünscht / Poolservice requested
7⁰⁰–7³⁰ | 7³⁰–8⁰⁰ | 8⁰⁰–8³⁰ | 8³⁰–9⁰⁰ | 9⁰⁰–9³⁰

Zimmer-Nr. | Kellner | Gedecke | Datum

Einfaches Frühstück mit:/Continental Breakfast with:

Kaffee / Coffee   Tee / Tea   Schokolade / Chocolate   Milch/Milk
  □   □   □   □ warm
                                                           □ kalt
                                                           □ Zitrone/lemon

Säfte/Juice
Orange □   Grapefruit □   Tomate □

□ ½ Grapefruit   □ Quark   □ natur
□ Bircher Müsli   □ Joghurt   □ mit Früchten

Eierspeisen/Egg Dishes
□ 1 gekochtes Ei / 1 boiled egg   □ Schinken / Ham
□ 2 Spiegeleier / 2 fried eggs mit/with □ Speck / Bacon
□ 2 Rühreier / 2 scrambled eggs   □ Würstchen / Sausages

□ Cornflakes □ Porridge □ mit Milch / with milk □ mit Sahne / with cream

Aufschnitt/Cold Cuts
□ Gekochter Schinken / Boiled ham   □ Roher Schinken / Smoked ham
□ Gemischter Aufschnitt / Selected cold cuts   □ Käse nach Wahl / Choice of cheeses

Preise sind auf der Etagenkarte vermerkt
Prices are noted on the menu
Gesamtsumme
Diese Preise sind Endpreise u. enth. Getränkesteuer, Bedieng u. MwSt
These prices are final & include Beverage Tax, Service Charge & V.A.T
Unterschrift

Besondere Wünsche/Special requests
Tageszeitung/Newspaper

Form 2

Anzahl der Gäste _____   Zimmer-Nummer _____
Name

BRISTOL HOTEL Kempinski Berlin

Mein Frühstuck um:/My breakfast at: am Pool gewünscht / Poolservice requested
7⁰⁰–7³⁰ | 7³⁰–8⁰⁰ | 8⁰⁰–8³⁰ | 8³⁰–9⁰⁰ | 9⁰⁰–9³⁰

Zimmer-Nr. | Kellner | Gedecke | Datum

Einfaches Frühstück mit:/Continental Breakfast with:

Kaffee / Coffee   Tee / Tea   Schokolade / Chocolate   Milch/Milk
  □   □   □   □ warm
                                                           □ kalt
                                                           □ Zitrone/lemon

Säfte/Juice
Orange □   Grapefruit □   Tomate □

□ ½ Grapefruit   □ Quark   □ natur
□ Bircher Müsli   □ Joghurt   □ mit Früchten

Eierspeisen/Egg Dishes
□ 1 gekochtes Ei / 1 boiled egg   □ Schinken / Ham
□ 2 Spiegeleier / 2 fried eggs mit/with □ Speck / Bacon
□ 2 Rühreier / 2 scrambled eggs   □ Würstchen / Sausages

□ Cornflakes □ Porridge □ mit Milch / with milk □ mit Sahne / with cream

Aufschnitt/Cold Cuts
□ Gekochter Schinken / Boiled ham   □ Roher Schinken / Smoked ham
□ Gemischter Aufschnitt / Selected cold cuts   □ Käse nach Wahl / Choice of cheeses

Preise sind auf der Etagenkarte vermerkt
Prices are noted on the menu
Gesamtsumme
Diese Preise sind Endpreise u. enth. Getränkesteuer, Bedieng u. MwSt
These prices are final & include Beverage Tax, Service Charge & V.A.T
Unterschrift

Besondere Wünsche/Special requests
Tageszeitung/Newspaper

STUDENT B   STUDENT B   STUDENT B   STUDENT B   STUDENT B

Arranging a business appointment B23

You are Herr Naumann, a local businessman. An associate of yours, Frau Richter, rings to try to fix a time at which you can both meet. You will need two hours for the meeting. Frau Naumann will also suggest times. If they are not possible, explain why. What time do you both decide on?

Februar/März	
27 So	abends → Frankfurt
28 Mo	Frankfurt
01 Di	12.00 zurück
02 Mi	9.00 – 12.00 Besuch v. Herrn Seidl (Wien)
03 Do	14.00 – 18.30 Konferenz
04 Fr	10.20 zum Flughafen → Paris
05 Sa	Paris

STUDENT B STUDENT B STUDENT B STUDENT B STUDENT B

B24 Sightseeing in Berlin

You work for the Berolina bus company in Berlin. A tourist rings to ask you about various sightseeing tours. Give information about the tours as follows: number of the tour; time(s); duration; cost. The tourist will tell you where he/she is telephoning from. Describe how to get from there to the starting-point for the tours.

Tour 6

Das Berlin der Kaiser, Könige und Kurfürsten
Historische West-Berlin-Tour 3½ Stunden

Eine Fahrt durch die Geschichte dieser Stadt, vorbei an den bekanntesten Sehenswürdigkeiten Berlins: Kaiser-Wilhelm-Gedächtniskirche, Diplomatenviertel, Brandenburger Tor, Reichstag, Kongreßhalle, Bellevue, Siegessäule, Schloß Charlottenburg (Führung), Belvedere, Mausoleum, Spandauer Altstadt, Zitadelle, Jagdschloß Grunewald (Führung), Glienicker Brücke
Wandeln Sie auf den Spuren brandenburgischer Kurfürsten, preußischer Könige und deutscher Kaiser. Fahren Sie an Orte und Plätze dieser Stadt, wo Geschichte gemacht wurde. Lassen Sie sich erzählen, welche Ereignisse und Personen mit den Straßennamen Berlins verbunden sind und erleben Sie eine Metropole, in der Gegenwart und Geschichte, Ost und West in deutlichem Kontrast stehen.
Entdecken Sie die Einmaligkeit Berlins.

Tour 7

Berlin bei Nacht 5 Stunden
nur samstags

Fluidum der Weltstadt im Lichterglanz! Erleben Sie diese einmalige Atmosphäre mit internationalem Publikum in den bekanntesten Bars und Nachtclubs. Sie sehen 3 bekannte Etablissements und deren erstklassige Programme. Im Preis enthalten sind Rundfahrt, Reiseleiter-Assistenz, Eintritt und das erste Getränk in jeder Bar. Die amüsante Nachtclubtour endet gegen 1.00 Uhr früh. Auch alleinreisende Damen sind herzlich willkommen. Platzreservierungen werden bis 20.00 Uhr erbeten. Abholung vom Hotel.

Tour 8

Potsdam – Sanssouci – Cecilienhof
Ganztagsfahrt (einschl. Mittagessen)
Halbtagsfahrt (einschl. Kaffeegedeck)

Stadtrundfahrt durch das alte und neue Potsdam. Besichtigung des weltbekannten Rokoko-Schlosses „Sanssouci". Führung durch das alte Kronprinzen-Palais „Schloß Cecilienhof" (Stätte des Potsdamer Abkommens von 1945). **Teilnahme an diesen Fahrten nur für Ausländer möglich.** Anmeldung unter Vorlage des Reisepasses bis 11.00 Uhr, bzw. am Vorabend.
Ganztagesfahrt:
Ab 1.5. jeden Dienstag, Donnerstag, Samstag
Abfahrt 9.30 Uhr, Rückkehr gegen 17.30 Uhr
Halbtagsfahrt:
Ab 1.5. jeden Mittwoch, Freitag, Sonntag
Abfahrt 13.00 Uhr, Rückkehr gegen 18.00 Uhr

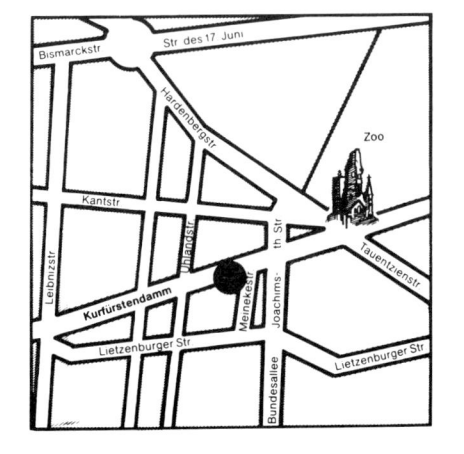

täglich/daily
Kurfürstendamm
Ecke Meinekestr.
bei Schultheiss
Bräuhaus

BEROLINA STADTRUNDFAHRTEN
SOMMERFAHRPLAN
vom 1.4. – 31.10.1984

Tour	Zeit			Std.	DM
1	9.00	West-Berlin-Tour	Sa/So – Sa/Su	2	19,–
8	9.30	Potsdam-Sanssouci, incl. Mittagessen/Lunch Di/Do/Sa – **nur für Ausländer –**		8	89,–
2	10.00	Große/Big West-Berlin-Tour		3	26,–
3	10.00	Ost-Berlin-Tour in German		3	27,–*
1	11.00	West-Berlin-Tour		2	19,–
5	11.00	Große Bus- und Schiffstour Big Tour West-Berlin by Bus and Boat Di/Tu – So/Su vom 1.5. – 30.9.1984		4½	27,–
8	13.00	Potsdam-Sanssouci, incl. Kaffeegedeck/coffee and cake Mi/Wed, Fr/Fr und So/Su		5	79,–
1	13.30	West-Berlin-Tour		2	19,–
3	14.00	Ost-Berlin-Tour incl. Pergamon-Museum		4	27,–*
6	14.00	Das Berlin der Kaiser, Könige u. Kurfürsten Historische West-Berlin-Tour – Sonntag – The Berlin of Emperors, Kings and Electors Historical West-Berlin-Tour – Sunday –		3½	29,–
2	14.30	Große/Big West-Berlin-Tour		3	26,–
1	16.00	West-Berlin-Tour		2	19,–
7	21.00	Berlin bei Nacht – Sonnabend – Berlin by night – Saturday –		5	99,–
4		Große kombinierte Stadtrundfahrt durch West- und Ost-Berlin. Individuelle Kombinationsmöglichkeit der Touren 1 oder 2 und 3. Die kombinierte Fahrkarte hat auch an mehreren Tagen Gültigkeit. **Zum Sparpreis** Big combined Sightseeing-Tour through West- and East-Berlin. Individual combination of Tours 1 or 2 and 3 possible. The combined ticket is also valid for different days.			43,–

STUDENT B   STUDENT B   STUDENT B   STUDENT B   STUDENT B

House-hunting

B25

You are house-hunting with your wife/husband and have only time to visit properties separately. You then ring each other to describe the houses you have looked at. Here is a plan of the bungalow you have been viewing. Ring your wife/husband and describe it it detail. He/she will make a quick sketch from your description which you can compare later.

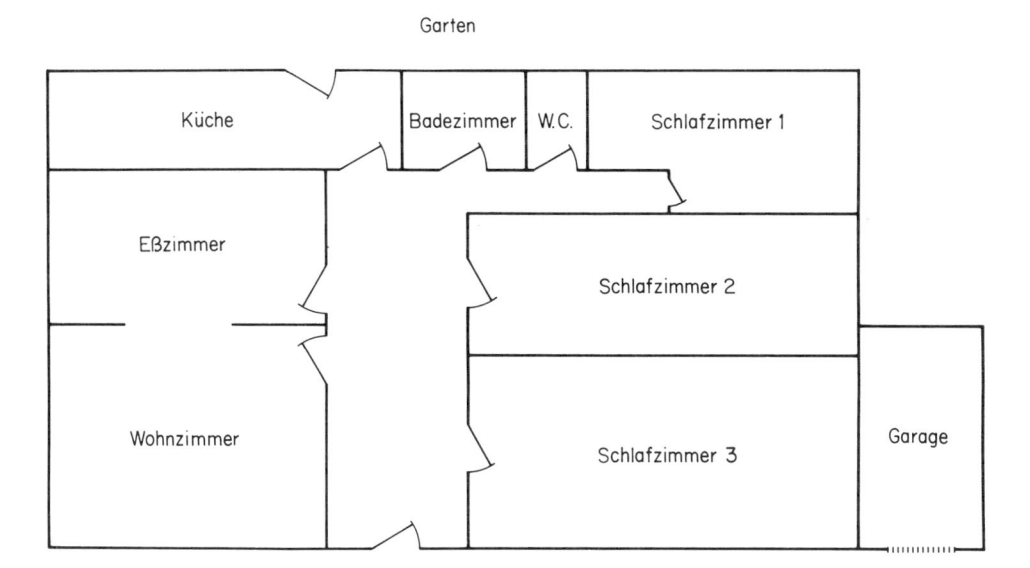

Garten

| Küche | Badezimmer | W.C. | Schlafzimmer 1 |

Eßzimmer

Schlafzimmer 2

Wohnzimmer

Schlafzimmer 3   Garage

B26 Theatre-going

You work for a theatre ticket agency in Berlin. A tourist rings to ask you various questions about theatre performances in the first half of July. Provide responses using the information below:

JULI		Deutsche Oper Berlin Bismarckstr. 34–37 Tel. 3 41 44 49	Schiller-Theater Bismarckstr. 110 Tel. 3 19 52 36	Schiller-Theater Werkstatt Bismarckstr. 110 Tel. 3 19 52 36	Schloßpark-Theater Schloßstr. 41 Tel. 7 91 12 13	Schaubühne am Lehniner Platz Kurfürstendamm 153 Tel. 89 00 23	Freie Volksbühne Schaperstr. 24 Tel. 8 81 37 42	Renaissance-Theater Hardenbergstr. 6 Tel. 3 12 42 02
1.	So	19.00 Orpheus in der Unterwelt	19.00 Komödie der Verführung	Keine Vorstellung	20.00 Stella	20.00 Cami	geschl. wegen Premierenvorbereitungen Ghetto	20.00 Die zwölf Geschworenen
2.	Mo	19.00 Orpheus in der Unterwelt	20.00 Eine Dummheit macht auch der Gescheiteste	20.00 Premiere: Ritt auf die Wartburg	20.00 Clavigo	Keine Vorstellung	geschl. wegen Premierenvorbereitungen Ghetto	20.00 Die zwölf Geschworenen
3.	Di	19.30 Simon Boccanegra (in ital. Sprache)	20.00 Leben Gundlings	Keine Vorstellung	20.00 Ich steig aus und mach'ne eigene Show	20.00 Cami	19.30 1. Voraufführung Ghetto	20.00 Die zwölf Geschworenen
4.	Mi	19.00 Die Zauberflöte	20.00 Furcht und Elend des Dritten Reiches	Keine Vorstellung	20.00 Einmal Moskau und zurück	20.00 Cami	19.30 2. Voraufführung Ghetto	20.00 Die zwölf Geschworenen
5.	Do	19.00 Ballettabend Schwanensee	19.00 Komödie der Verführung	20.00 Innere Stimmen	19.00 Trilogie der Ferienzeit	20.00 Cami	19.30 Premiere Ghetto	20.00 Die zwölf Geschworenen
6.	Fr	19.30 Simon Boccanegra (in ital. Sprache)	20.00 Amadeus	Keine Vorstellung	20.00 Phädra	Keine Vorstellung	19.30 Ghetto	20.00 Die zwölf Geschworenen
7.	Sa	19.00 Ballettabend, 21.30 Ravel-Ballettabend	20.00 Ein Sommernachtstraum	Keine Vorstellung	20.00 Einmal Moskau und zurück	Keine Vorstellung	19.30 Ghetto	20.00 Die zwölf Geschworenen
8.	So	11.00 Sinfoniekonz. 17.00 + 20.00 Ballett 21.00 Metropol: Pr. E. Sommernachtstr.	20.00 Ein Sommernachtstraum	Keine Vorstellung	20.00 Einmal Moskau und zurück	Keine Vorstellung	19.30 Ghetto	20.00 Die zwölf Geschworenen
9.	Mo	19.30 Simon Boccanegra (i. ital. Spr.) 21.00 Metropol: Ein Sommernachtstr.	20.00 Eine Dummheit macht auch der Gescheiteste	20.00 Ritt auf die Wartburg	20.00 Der Botschafter	Keine Vorstellung	Keine Vorstellung	20.00 Die zwölf Geschworenen
10.	Di	19.00 Orpheus in der Unterwelt	20.00 Eine Dummheit macht auch der Gescheiteste	20.00 Tucholsky in Rock	20.00 Clavigo	Keine Vorstellung	19.30 Ghetto	20.00 Die zwölf Geschworenen
11.	Mi	19.00 Orpheus i. d. Unterwelt, 21.00 Metropol: E. Sommernachtstraum	20.00 Furcht und Elend des Dritten Reiches	20.00 Tucholsky in Rock	20.00 Einmal Moskau und zurück	Keine Vorstellung	19.30 Ghetto	20.00 Die zwölf Geschworenen
12.	Do	19.30 Simon Boccanegra (i. ital. Spr.) 21.00 Metropol: E. Sommernachtstraum	20.00 Leben Gundlings	Keine Vorstellung	19.00 Trilogie der Ferienzeit	Keine Vorstellung	19.30 Ghetto	
13.	Fr	Theaterferien	20.00 Der Schein trugt	20.00 Innere Stimmen	19.00 Trilogie der Ferienzeit	Keine Vorstellung	19.30 Ghetto	
14.	Sa	Theaterferien	19.00 Premiere: Die Jungfrau von Orleans	20.00 Ein Stück Monolog	20.00 Clavigo	Keine Vorstellung	19.30 Ghetto	
15.	So	Theaterferien	19.00 Die Jungfrau von Orleans	20.00 Ritt auf die Wartburg	20.00 Einmal Moskau und zurück	Keine Vorstellung	19.30 Ghetto	
16.	Mo	Theaterferien	19.00 Der Hauptmann von Köpenick	Keine Vorstellung	20.00 Krankheit der Jugend	Theaterferien	Keine Vorstellung	Keine Vorstellung

STUDENT B   **STUDENT B**   **STUDENT B**   **STUDENT B**   **STUDENT B**

Planning a train journey   **B27**

1. You are a clerk in the information office at the railway station in Kiel. A traveller asks you about the times of various trains. Provide the information from your copy of the timetable below:

[Timetable: Nach Düsseldorf und zurück — fares 1. Kl 129,00 / 2. Kl 86,00 / 258,00 / 172,00]

Zug	Kiel ab	Bemerkungen	Düsseldorf an	Zug	Düsseldorf ab	Bemerkungen	Kiel an
2171	5.02	① bis ⑤, ⑥; ⑪ Neum, Hamburg Hbf	10.28	D 235	3.58	⑪ Hamburg Hbf	9.57
E3501	5.57	① bis ⑥, ⑧; u Dortmund	11.28	631	5.57	① bis ⑤, ⑥; ⑪ Altona	11.22
				635	7.27	① bis ⑤, ⑥; ⑪ Hmb Hbf	12.39
				543	8.27	① bis ⑥, ⑧; ⑪ Dortmund u Hmb-Altona	13.40
613	7.00	① bis ⑥, ⑧; ⑪ Dortmund	12.28	637	9.27	⑪ Hmb-Altona	14.57
3509	7.59	⑦; ⑪ Altona	13.28	133	10.27	⑪ Hmb Hbf	15.55
3515	8.46	① bis ⑥, ⑧; ⑪ Hmb-Altona	14.28	535	11.27	⑪ Altona	16.56
D 927	10.19	① bis ⑥, ⑧;	15.28	626	12.27	⑪ Dortmund u Hmb-Altona	↑17.57 / ×18.15
E3521	11.06	⑪ Neumünster u Hamburg Hbf	16.28	614	13.27	⑪ Hamburg Hbf u Neumünster	↑19.04 / a 19.13
E3519	×12.00	⑪ Hmb-Altona u Dortmund	17.28	518	14.27	⑪ Hmb-Altona	20.09
D 589	13.01	täglich außer ⑥, ⑧; ⊠	18.28	108	15.27	⑪ Hmb-Altona	21.05
				526	16.27	täglich außer ⑥, ⑧; ⑪ Dortmund u Altona	22.08
E3525	13.50	⑪ Hmb-Altona	19.28	612	17.27		22.50
693	15.12	täglich außer ⑥, ⑧;	20.28	1516	17.59	⑦, ⑪, ⑪ Neumünster	23.45
				516	18.27	tägl auß ⑥, ⑧; ⑪ Hmb Hbf	0.18
E3535	16.03	⑪ Hmb-Altona u Dortmund	21.28	620	19.27	⑦, ⑪, ⑪ Dortmund u Hamburg Hbf	0.50
E3537	17.04	täglich außer ⑥, ⑧;	22.28	506	20.27	⑦, ⑧; ⑪ Hamburg Hbf	1.52
E3541	18.04	⑪ Hmb-Altona	23.28	D 233	23.07	⑦, ⑧; ⑪ Hmb Hbf	4.40
E 838	21.34	täglich außer ⑥, ⑨	4.54	D 839	23.59	täglich außer ⑥, ⑧; bis Neumünster	8.20

[Timetable: Nach Essen Hbf und zurück — fares 1. Kl 122,00 / 2. Kl 81,00 / 244,00 / 162,00]

Zug	Kiel ab	Bemerkungen	Essen Hbf an	Zug	Essen Hbf ab	Bemerkungen	Kiel an
2171	5.02	① bis ⑤, ⑥; ⑪ Neum, Hmb Hbf u Dortmund	10.00	D 839	0.43	① bis ⑤, ⑥; bis Neumünster	8.20
E3501	5.57	① bis ⑥, ⑧; ⑪ Hmb-Altona	11.00	D 235	4.26	⑪ Hamburg Hbf	9.57
613	7.00	① bis ⑥, ⑧; ⑪ Dortmund	12.00	631	6.24	① bis ⑤, ⑥; ⑪ Altona	11.22
3509	7.59	⑦; ⑪ Altona	13.00	635	7.54	① bis ⑤, ⑥; ⑪ Hmb Hbf	12.39
3515	8.46	⑪ Hmb-Altona	14.00	543	8.54	① bis ⑥, ⑧; ⑪ Dortmund	13.40
D 927	10.19	① bis ⑥, ⑧; ⑪ Hamburg Hbf	15.00	637	9.54	⑪ Hmb-Altona	14.57
E3521	11.06	⑪ Neum, Hmb Hbf	16.00	133	10.54	⑪ Hmb Hbf	15.55
E3519	×12.00	⑪ Hmb-Altona u Dortmund	17.00	535	11.54	⑪ Altona	16.56
				626	12.54	⑪ Dortmund u Hmb-Altona	↑17.57 / ×18.15
D 589	13.01	täglich außer ⑥, ⑧; ⊠ ⑪ Hmb-Altona	18.00	614	13.54	⑪ Hamburg Hbf u Neumünster	a 19.04 / c 19.13
E3525	13.50	⑪ Hmb-Altona	19.00	518	14.54	⑪ bis ⑤, ⑥; ⑪ Altona	20.09
693	15.12	täglich außer ⑥, ⑧; ⑪ Hmb-Altona	20.00	108	15.54	⑪ Hmb-Altona	21.05
				526	16.54	täglich außer ⑥, ⑧; ⑪ Dortmund u Altona	22.08
E3535	16.03	⑪ Hmb-Altona u Dortmund	21.00	612	17.54		22.50
E3537	17.04	täglich außer ⑥, ⑧; ⑪ Hmb-Altona	22.00	1516	18.26	⑦, ⑧; ⑪ Neumünster	23.45
				516	18.54	tägl auß ⑥, ⑧; ⑪ Hmb Hbf	0.18
E3541	18.04	⑪ Hmb-Altona	23.00	620	19.54	⑦, ⑧; ⑪ Dortmund u Hamburg Hbf	0.50
E 838	21.34		4.18	506	20.54	⑦, ⑧; ⑪ Hamburg Hbf	1.52
				D 233	23.37	⑦, ⑧; ⑪ Hmb Hbf	4.40

a = ✗ außer ⑥
c = ⑦ und +
① = nicht 25. bis 27. XII., 1. bis 3. I. u 10. bis 12. IV.
② = nicht 24. u 27. XII., 31. XII. bis 3. I. u 8. bis 12. IV.
③ = nicht 2. I. u 10. IV.
④ = nicht 25. u 26. XII., 1., 2. I., 10. u 11. IV.
⑤ = nicht 18. XI., 25. u 26. XII., 1. I. u 12. IV.
⑥ = nicht 24. bis 26. XII., 31. XII. bis 2. I. u 8. bis 11. IV.
⑦ = auch 22. V., nicht 24. bis 26. XII., 31. XII., 8. bis 11. IV.
⑧ = auch ⑦ IX., nicht 25. bis 27. XII., 1. I. u 10. bis 12. IV.
⑨ = auch 1. V., nicht 24., 25. u 31. XII., 1. I. u 12. IV.
⑩ = auch 12. u 13. IV., nicht 11. IV.
⑪ = auch 18. XI., 28. XII., 4. I., 12. u 13. IV., 22. u 23. I., 12. u 13. IV., nicht 11. IV.
⑫ = auch 18. XI., 28. XII., 4. I., 12. u 13. IV., nicht 11. IV.

2. You are at the information office in the railway station in Kiel and wish to find out the following information:

     – which trains leave Flensburg for Kiel before 7.00 am?

     – which train would you need to catch in order to arrive in Flensburg by midday?

     – is there an afternoon InterCity train from Kiel which would get you to Hamburg-Altona by 4.00 pm?

     – how may InterCity trains are there daily from Hamburg Hauptbahnhof to Kiel and how long does the journey take?

Ask the appropriate questions and record the information below:

Reiseverbindungen   Connections   Horaires des trains   **DB**

Station	Reisetag/Wochentag date/day date/jour	Uhr time heure	Uhr time heure	Uhr time heure	Bemerkungen notes observations / Auskunft ohne Gewähr information without guarantee renseignements non garantis
	ab dep				
	an arr				
	ab dep				
	an arr				
	ab dep				
	an arr				
	ab dep				
	an arr				
	ab dep				
	an arr				

STUDENT B

B28 Making a *Sachertorte*

Your friend rings to say that he/she has just made a disastrous Viennese chocolate cake, a *Sachertorte*. He/she wants to check the ingredients with you to discover where things went wrong. You happen to have a copy of Marianne Piepenstock's recipe book *Österreichische Küche* and you look up the recipe. Correct the information that your friend will give you.

Sachertorte

6 Eier, 160 g Butter, 160 g Zucker, 175 g Schokolade,
1 TL Vanillepuder oder 1 Päckchen Vanillezucker,
Marillenmarmelade, Schokoladenglasur, 160 g Mehl

100 g Zucker, Butter und die im Wasserbad erwärmte Schokolade schaumig rühren, nach 5 Minuten Rühren die Eidotter zufügen. Eiweiß mit 60 g Zucker sehr steif schlagen, dann beide Massen mischen und Mehl mit Vanillezucker langsam einrühren. In eine gut gebutterte Springform füllen und bei milder Hitze langsam backen. Dann einmal durchschneiden, mit Aprikosenmarmelade füllen, oben und auf den Seiten bestreichen und darüber Schokoladenglasur geben.

Schokoladenglasur:
125 g Puderzucker und 2 EL Wasser aufkochen, bis sich Faden ziehen lassen, 100 g im Wasserbad erwärmte Schokolade darunterrühren, bis die Masse völlig glatt ist, auf die Torte gießen, Oberseite und Ränder müssen bedeckt sein.

STUDENT B   STUDENT B   STUDENT B   STUDENT B   STUDENT B

A trip to Munich

B29

You are a teacher in a German school. A British colleague rings to ask you about Munich (the city in which you teach) since he/she is planning to bring over a group of pupils. You have to provide information about the places most worth visiting. Describe where each of them is and say a little about why they are interesting.

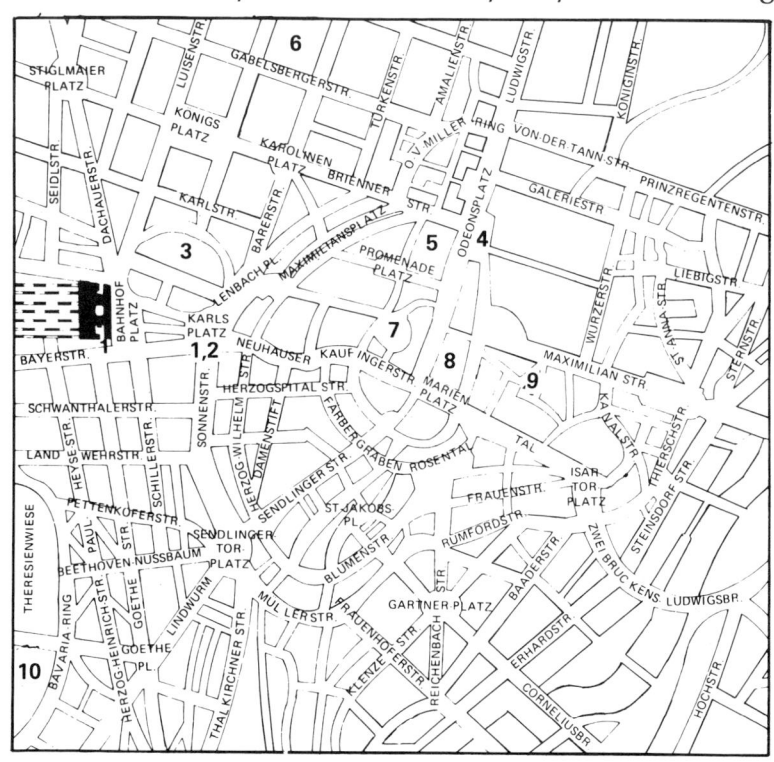

1. *Karlstor* Teil der alten Befestigungsanlage.
2. *Justizpalast* Im neubarocken Stil erbaut.
3. *Botanischer Garten* 1909-14 angelegt.
4. *Feldherrnhalle* 1841-44 erbaut.
5. *Theatinerkirche* Ehemalige Hofkirche der bayerischen Kurfürsten.
6. *Alte Pinakothek* Sehr wichtige Gemäldegalerie, weltweit bekannt, eine der besten Gemäldesammlungen, die es überhaupt gibt.
7. *Frauenkirche* Der Dom Münchens, eigentlich Dom und Pfarrkirche Unserer Lieben Frau, stammt aus dem 15. Jahrhundert, jetzt Wahrzeichen Münchens.
8. *Rathaus* Der alte Bau (1470) wurde im Krieg zerstört und später wieder aufgebaut.
9. *Hofbräuhaus* Musik und viel, viel Bier! Schöner Innenhof.
10. *Bavaria* 30 m hoch, Mitte des 19. Jahrhunderts, Personifizierung Bayerns. Man kann dieses Riesendenkmal im Innern besteigen – es gibt nur 130 Stufen!

STUDENT B   STUDENT B   STUDENT B   STUDENT B   STUDENT B

B30 Registering a change of address

You work in the town hall of a small German town, Ludwigshausen. One of your duties is to record the details of people who have just moved to the town and have to complete their *Anmeldebestätigung*. Since you are not very busy at the moment you decide to complete the necessary form for Herr Herzberg, who has just arrived in your office. Ask him the questions that will enable you to fill in the details.

Anmeldebestätigung

Folgende Personen sind heute bei der unterzeichneten Meldebehörde angemeldet worden als wohnhaft in:

Neue Wohnung *Bisherige Wohnung*
Tag des Einzugs: Anschrift:
Anschrift:
           8463 LUDWIGSHAUSEN

Familienname (bei Frauen auch Geburtsname)	Vornamen (sämtliche, Rufnamen unterstreichen)	Geburtstag -monat, -jahr
1.	....	....
2.	....	....
3.	....	....
4.	....	....
5.	....	....

Geburtsort (falls Ausland, Staat angeben)	Beruf	Familienstand (led., verh., verw., gesch.)	Staatsangehörigkeit
1.	....	....	....
2.	....	....	....
3.	....	....	....
4.	....	....	....
5.	....	....	....

Unterschrift des Anmeldenden

....
Ludwigshausen, den .... 19 ......   Ludwigshausen, den .... 19 ......
                                        Stadt Ludwigshausen
                                        Meldebehörde

                                        I.A. ....
                                        (Unterschrift)